The Coast Guard
ON THE TEXAS BORDER

JACKIE KYGER

THE
History
PRESS

Published by The History Press
Charleston, SC
www.historypress.com

Copyright © 2021 by Jackie Kyger
All rights reserved

Photographs courtesy of the U.S. Coast Guard Historian's Office and private collections.

First published 2021

Manufactured in the United States

ISBN 9781467150125

Library of Congress Control Number: 2021938573

*To all those who have served in the U.S. Coast Guard on the Texas border. May
your military service be remembered for the history that you made.*

Blessed are they that go down to the sea in ships, that do business in great waters.
—Psalm 107:23 KJV

Contents

Acknowledgements

No one historian works in a vacuum, and a sole interest does not document history—it takes a team. I want to thank the following people and acknowledge the resources that proved very valuable in creating this historical collection.

First, I would like to thank fellow Arcadia Publishing author Valerie Bates, whose book *Images of America: Port Isabel* served as a point of inspiration—a note of gratitude for Valerie's passion for history, encouragement and local historical connections.

A special thanks to the commanding officer of Coast Guard Station South Padre Island LCDR Daniel Ippolito, USCG. His generous permission to access and include the URG-Historic Context Study of the United States Coast Guard in Sector Corpus Christi from Port Aransas South to the Rio Grande, Brownsville, Texas, and the station's image archives was a huge assist in bringing this work to completion. The future of the Coast Guard is in great hands!

The images and information in this book have been gleaned and culled from private collections and public digital archives, oral histories and embellished sea stories. A special thanks to the following:

- Coast Guard Historian Publications and Digital Archives Office
- Foundation for Coast Guard History
- URG-Historic Context Study of the Coast Guard
- National Archives

Acknowledgements

- Texas Historical Commission
- Museums of Port Isabel
- Valarie Bates
- Andrew Dart
- LCDR Charles Wilson, USCG (retired)
- LCDR Daniel Ippolito, USCG (active)
- LT Alan Grodecki, USCG (retired)
- CWO3 Dave Cook, USCG (retired)
- BMCM Jim Caldwell, USCG (retired)
- ETCM Bill Dietz, USCG (retired)
- BMCS Luis Canales, USCG (retired)
- BMC John Epps, USCG (retired)
- ETC Elias Degaspri, USCG (retired)
- MK1 J.E. Taylor, USCG (active)
- PSC Arnulfo V. Martinez, USCG (retired)
- PSC Francisco "J.C." Chapa, USCG (retired)
- SK3/YN3 Dora Eason, USCG (retired)
- BM3 Lili Valle (Alvarez), USCG (veteran)

Bravo Zulu—for your timeless, tireless and heartfelt contributions!

Introduction

T he Rio Grande River is a natural boundary between the United States and Mexico, and it gets its earliest known recorded history from the sixteenth century. In 1519, Spanish conquistador and cartographer Alfonso Álvarez de Pineda navigated from the Gulf of Mexico and entered the mouth of a river that would eventually become a historically significant natural boundary. Making his way upriver, he was so impressed by all the palmetto trees growing along the banks that he named the river Rio de Las Palmas. In modern times, it is called the Rio Grande River, and it marks the ending of the area of responsibility (AOR) for the United States Coast Guard's southernmost station, located on South Padre Island, Texas.

The Brazos Santiago Pass is located six nautical miles north of the Rio Grande River. It was a natural inlet between the Gulf of Mexico and the Laguna Madre Bay. Little more is known about this area prior to the sixteenth century, other than the belief that a Native tribe thrived here.

While it is not known exactly who named the Pass, Brazos Santiago "Arms of Saint James," the naming is believed to have occurred between 1520 and 1525, when Spanish explorers navigated through the pass and safely dropped anchor in the sheltered waters of the Laguna Madre Bay. This likely marked the beginning of navigation to the area. The pass is the southernmost natural inlet that allows mariners access to shelter from the Gulf of Mexico. Today, it is still the southernmost pass, but it is no longer considered a natural inlet, as dredging and the creation of jetties have prevented the natural inlet from silting into a non-navigable state. It remains, to this day, an important area to the United States.

The Brazos Santiago Pass lies between Brazos Island and South Padre Island within Cameron County, Texas. The county was established on February 12, 1948, with the town of Santa Rita being its first county seat. The area comprised more than three thousand square miles. In 1852, a western portion of the county was renamed Hidalgo County. In 1912, a large northern track was renamed Willacy County. Today, Cameron County comprises approximately nine hundred square miles, of which the Brazos Santiago Pass has remained a part since the county was established in 1948.

The United States Coast Guard has a long history of service, dating back to the revenue cutter days of 1790. With the exception of icebreaking operations, the Coast Guard has performed every mission along this nation's southernmost Texas boundary. Its earliest presence in South Texas was in response to the aids to navigation mission, lighting the way for the mariner.

In 1789, the first Congress of the United States created and passed the act to formally support navigation aids through the establishment of lighthouses. But it would be another sixty-three years before a lighthouse would appear on the horizon of South Texas.

In 1836, Texas became a state, and in 1851, the construction of the Port Isabel lighthouse began. Once completed, the lighthouse became the southernmost navigation beacon in the mainland of the United States.

Beginning in 1875, Congress directed the secretary of the treasury to acquire the right to use and build sites for lifesaving and lifeboat stations. This led to government land being established in the Brazos Santiago Pass area of South Texas. The United States Life-Saving Service was created in 1878. The first station in the area was located on Brazos Santiago Island.

On January 28, 1915, President Woodrow Wilson signed a bill merging the U.S. Life-Saving Service and the U.S. Revenue Cutter Service, creating the United States Coast Guard. The U.S. Coast Guard has been here for hundreds of years. This is our story.

1

U.S. Lighthouse Service

1789-1939

Alexander Hamilton, the secretary of the treasury in 1789, created within the Department of Treasury the U.S. Lighthouse Service. This was done to formally establish a federal aids to navigation system of marking the channels and lighting the way for mariners. Before, this was left in the hands of state and local volunteer groups.

In 1850, the U.S. government was considering the best location for a lighthouse in South Texas. Both the Point Isabel area and Brazos Santiago were being considered, but ultimately, the decision was made to utilize Army-controlled property in the Point Isabel area.

THE LIFESAVING AND RESCUE BOATS ASSIGNED ALONG THE TEXAS BORDER (1850–PRESENT)

Surfboats, in the early days of the lifesaving service, were easy to launch from the beach and were propelled by oars. Motor lifeboats added range and speed to the rescues in the early 1900s, and the styles changed over the years. In the 1960s, the forty-four-foot-long motor lifeboat (MLB) became the heavy weather rescue standard. The forty-four-foot-long MLB is actually forty-four feet and one and a half inches long, with a beam of twelve feet and eight inches and a draft of three feet and two inches. Twin diesel engines power the MLB for a maximum speed between thirteen and fifteen knots. In 1967, Coast Guard Station Port Isabel was chosen to receive 1 of the

110 MLBs that were to be produced. A boat crew from Station Port Isabel was sent to the Coast Guard shipyard in Curtis Bay, Maryland, to receive MLB 44395. The Texas crew navigated the lifeboat from Maryland to its homeport on South Padre Island, Texas.

The following rescue boats have protected the Brazos Santiago Pass and Texas border:

1850: Francis type metallic pulling surfboat (in the custody of the local collector of customs).

1882: Twenty-seven-foot-long branch-type pulling surfboat.

1884: Twenty-two-foot-long supply sloop.
Ten-foot-long skiff.

1887: Fifteen-foot-long skiff.

1889: Sloop (transferred from Station Saluria).

1894: Twenty-three-foot-long Monomoy-type pulling surfboat.

1899: Twenty-six-foot-long Monomoy-type pulling surfboat (transferred from Station Sabine Pass).

1909: Beebe-McLellan-type pulling/sailing surfboat, no. 909.

1915: Beebe-McLellan-type motor surfboat, no. 1566.

1919: Thirty-six-foot-long type H motor lifeboat, no. 2164.

1924: Thirty-six-foot-long cabin picket boat, no. 2311/CG36301 (later transferred to Station Aransas).
Thirty-six-foot-long cabin picket boat, no. 2340.

1925: Type H motor lifeboat, no. 2164.

1927: Type H pulling/sailing surfboat, no. 3241.

1930s: Type H motor lifeboat, no. 1566 (transferred from Station Cape Cod Canal).

1934: Type S motor surfboat, no. 4412/CG25548.

1935: Type SR pulling surfboat, no. 4737/CG25434.

1939: Thirty-six-foot-long type TRS motor lifeboat, no. 5168/CG36434.
Thirty-six-foot-long type TRS motor lifeboat, no. 5191/CG36452.

1942: Thirty-eight-foot-long cabin picket boat, no. 4231/CG38435.

1943: Cabin motorboat, no. 8781/CG25704.
World War II: Thirty-eight-foot-long cabin picket boat, no. 4334/CG38438.

1947: Type SR motor surfboat, CG25947.

1952: Forty-foot-long utility boat, large, CG40502.

1960s: Forty-foot-long utility boats, large, CG40504 (transferred from PSSTA Houston) and CG40530.

1969: Forty-four-foot-long motor lifeboat, CG44395.

The Crew of CG 40530 underway in dress white "Cracker Jack" uniform and on patrol. *USCG Station South Padre Island (SPI) Collection.*

Coast Guard Motor Lifeboat 44395 moored at Station Port Isabel. The CGC *Point Nowell* is in the background as "dress ship" (nautical flags hoisted). *USCG Station SPI Collection.*

Coast Guard Utility Boat 41390 with its engine hatches open. CG 44395 is in the background, moored at Station Port Isabel. *USCG Station SPI Collection.*

1972: Forty-foot-long utility boat, large, CG40475 (transferred from another station).

1974: Forty-one-foot-long utility boat, large, CG41323.

1980: Forty-one-foot-long utility boat, large, CG41468.
Forty-one-foot-long utility boat, large, CG41390.

1990s: Twenty-one-foot-long utility boat, (RHIB) CG213514.

1997: Twenty-seven-foot-long utility boat, small, (RHIB) CG279503 (Operation Gulf Shield).
Twenty-seven-foot-long special purpose craft (fiberglass hull), CG279501 (Operation Gulf Shield).
Twenty-seven-foot-long special purpose craft (fiberglass hull), CG279502 (Operation Gulf Shield).
Twenty-seven-foot-long special purpose craft (fiberglass hull), CG279503 (Operation Gulf Shield).

1999: Twelve-foot-long skiff, CG123502.

Top: A jet stream propulsion (no propeller) twenty-five-foot-long rigged hull inflatable boat patrolling the entrance to the Brazos Santiago Channel. *Author's collection*.

Bottom: Underway with the Boy Scouts of America's Sea Explorers (BSA SE). The Station Port Isabel was a BSA SE sponsor for several years. *Author's collection*.

2000s: Twenty-seven-foot-long special purpose craft, CG273058.
Twenty-seven-foot-long special purpose craft, CG273059.
Twenty-seven-foot-long special purpose craft, CG273010.
Twelve-foot-long skiff, CG123502.
Eighteen-foot-long skiff, CG183569.

2003: Forty-seven-foot-long motor lifeboat, CG47315 (later transferred to another station).

2007: Twenty-three-foot-long special purpose craft, shallow water, CG232517.

2008: Forty-one-foot-long utility boat, large, CG41362 (transferred from another station).
Thirty-three-foot-long special purpose craft, law enforcement, CG33105.

Top: Several Coast Guard fast response boats and the forty-one-foot-long UTB boat standing by for an emergency in the Station Port Isabel's covered moorings. *USCG Station SPI Collection.*

Bottom: A multipurpose fast response boat for search-and-rescue and law enforcement missions along the Texas border. *Author's Collection.*

Thirty-three-foot-long special purpose craft, law enforcement, CG33106.
Thirty-three-foot-long special purpose craft, law enforcement, CG33107.
Twenty-four-foot-long special purpose craft, shallow water, CG24505.
Twenty-four-foot-long special purpose craft, shallow water, CG24506.
2009: Forty-one-foot-long utility boat, large, CG41468 (transferred from another station).

2010: Forty-one-foot-long utility boat, large, CG41482 (transferred from another station).

2012: Thirty-three-foot-long special purpose craft, law enforcement, CG33122.

Thirty-three-foot-long special purpose craft, law enforcement, CG33124.

2014: Forty-five-foot-long response boats, medium, CG45748.

Forty-five-foot-long response boats, medium, CG45750.

2015: Thirty-three-foot-long special purpose craft, law enforcement, CG33141 (transferred from another station).

THE POINT ISABEL LIGHTHOUSE (1852)

While the lighthouse stands in the busy part of Port Isabel today, when it was built in 1852, there was little in the way of a town, and what was there certainly would not be considered busy. The property chosen for the lighthouse location was on the U.S. Army facility Fort Polk. The contractor was a local Brownsville builder, and it took a year for the contractor to complete the project.

The Port Isabel Lighthouse stands towering above the city as a reminder of the Coast Guard's watch-keeping duties and deep-rooted history in South Texas. *USCG Station SPI collection.*

In 1851, ground was broken, and funds were provided by Congress to build the Point Isabel Lighthouse. The forefathers of the Coast Guard were lighthouse keepers and had a rich history in aids to navigation. The construction of the Point Isabel Lighthouse took two years to complete, and it began "watching properly" in 1853. Once completed, it stood eighty-two feet tall, and the beacon, in its finest hour, was visible for approximately sixteen miles across the Laguna Madre and out into the Gulf of Mexico. Being located on Army property, the lighthouse keeper lived in Army quarters until a dedicated family home was built near the lighthouse in 1855. In 1952, the Point Isabel Lighthouse was designated a Texas State Historical Site.

BRAZOS SANTIAGO LIGHTHOUSE (1878)

The Brazos Santiago Pass, while it was a natural inlet leading from the Gulf of Mexico to the southern end of the Laguna Madre, was not a particularly easy area to navigate. Many sailors would rely on dead reckoning navigation skills to find the general location of the pass. Once there, if visibility were clear, the lookout in the crow's nest of the ship could see Santa Ysabel's Bluffs. Seeing the bluffs was a visual cue that the ship was nearing the Brazos Santiago Pass, an area known as "El Fronton." In later times, it would be renamed Port Isabel, Texas.

A ship-pilot station, utilizing flags in 1847, assisted ships through the passage and across the sand bars of the Brazos Santiago Pass. This limited the ships to daytime and clear visibility assistance. In 1853, the Brazos Santiago Beacon, a wooden tower mounted on wheels, was put into service. The beacon served as a front-range light, aligning behind it with the newly created Point Isabel Lighthouse. Mariners offshore could maneuver their ships so that the Point Isabel Lighthouse was directly atop and vertical to the Brazos Santiago Beacon. That alignment would be the preferred steering course for entering the natural inlet of the Brazos Santiago Pass. While the beacon need not be on wheels, a land agreement could not be reached for it to be permanently installed, so a mobile solution was the best at the time—they kept it mobile so as not to offend any of the landowners.

In 1854, a more permanent non-moveable wooden lighthouse was constructed. Due to weather and salt air abuse, it was rebuilt in 1864. This proved temporary, as did other attempts over the next few years, and in 1878, the iron screw-pile-base Brazos Santiago Lighthouse was built. And

The waterfront facility at Station Port Isabel. A beacon is mounted on top of it, and to the left is what remains of the Brazos-Santiago Lighthouse. *LCDR C.R. Wilson's collection.*

while buildings on the platform came and went due to storms and fires, the iron screw-pile frame remained in place for more than one hundred years.

In 1939, it was outfitted with electricity and an electric beacon. In the following year, 1940, a fire burned the wooden structure of the lighthouse, destroying the light. A temporary light was mounted to the remaining screw-pile structure. In 1942, the lighthouse beacon was relocated to the top of the Station Point Isabel Boathouse, approximately one hundred feet from the screw-pilings location. While there is mention of Brazos Santiago and Point Isabel, the Brazos Santiago Lighthouse was physically located on the southern end of South Padre Island, Texas.

In 1951, on Labor Day weekend, a fire broke out, destroying the boathouse and the beacon. It was then decided to move the beacon to the Coast Guard station's main building. It was mounted in the widow-watch, the station's uppermost lookout platform, where it remained, watching properly, until the building was abandoned in the mid-1970s. The local ship pilots built a small pilot station on top of the iron screw-piles, and piloting operations were based there for a few years. In the late 1980s, the iron screw-piles were removed by a maritime contractor. At extreme low tide, its base can still be seen.

Today, the Point Isabel Lighthouse remains a historic reminder of the Coast Guard's preceding agency—the U.S. Lighthouse Service. In modern

Above: West side of the waterfront facility, taken from the station. A three-hundred-yard walkway on the right runs between the station and the waterfront. *LCDR C.R. Wilson's collection.*

Left: Brownsville Ship Channel, front range. Light and day boards line up below the rear range to aid ships coming in from the sea buoy. *MK1 J.E. Taylor's collection.*

Brownsville Ship Channel, rear range. Light and day boards line up above the front range to aid ships coming in from the sea buoy. *MK1 J.E. Taylor's collection.*

times, the Brazos Santiago Pass entrance lights the way for mariners with Coast Guard navigational channel range lights and red and green entrance buoy lights marking the north and south jetties. One and a half miles offshore is the Brazos Santiago Sea Buoy, which alerts mariners that jetties and landfall are near. It is painted with red and white stripes, with a spherical shape on top of it. It has a white light that blinks the Morse code signal to distinguish it from other background lights from shore. The Morse signal pattern is a short blink followed by a long blink (- —). The sea buoy is much easier to locate than the Port Isabel bluffs, as, in modern times, the bluffs are lost to the city skyline of South Padre Island when approaching from the sea.

QUARANTINE STATION (1882)

As a result of the 1870 Texas Quarantine Act, stations were established along the south Texas Gulf Coast. The quarantine stations' purpose was to provide a safe location for those infected with yellow fever and cholera. Concerns

The quarantine station's hexagonal shape and stilts were standard design features for the many types of stations along the Texas coast. *USCG Station SPI collection.*

with quarantine date back to the revenue cutter days. In 1796, Congress passed an act requiring the revenue cutters to aid in the management of quarantining and each state's health laws. In 1798, the Congressional Act for the Relief of Sick and Disabled Seamen was approved. As a result, the

United States Marine Hospital Service (MHS), later known as the Public Health Service, was created.

In 1825, Congress empowered the revenue cutter service to enforce state quarantine laws. In 1878, the MHS was given quarantine authority.

In 1882, a stilted wooden octagonal-shaped quarantine station with ample window ventilation and shutters was built near the Brazos Santiago Lighthouse. It is believed that its approximate location was in the area of the modern-day Sea Ranch Marina on South Padre Island. Ships and boats desiring to come into the Brazos Santiago Pass were first inspected at sea. If any signs of yellow fever or cholera were found, the ship would be directed to anchor and remain at sea in quarantine status. The nautical signal flag "Quebec," an all-yellow flag, would be flown, indicating that the ship had been placed in quarantine. In modern times, it means the opposite; flying the "Quebec" flag indicates the vessel is free of any disease and is requesting to enter the harbor.

2
U.S. Revenue Cutter Service
1790-1915

In 1790, one year after the U.S. Lighthouse Service was formed under Secretary of the Treasury Alexander Hamilton, Congress passed the Tariff Act, creating, within the Treasury Department, the U.S. Revenue Cutter Service, with a fleet of ten cutters. The revenue cutter service was intended to protect the United States from smugglers and provide revenue through import tax enforcement—hence the name U.S. Revenue Cutter Service.

In 1846, in the area of the Brazos Santiago Pass, as a result of a border dispute between Mexico and the United States, a line was drawn by General Zachary Taylor, and it ended at the mouth of the Rio Grande River. On May 13, 1846, President James Polk signed a declaration of war against Mexico, and revenue cutters were put into service in the Gulf of Mexico. This fleet was a combination of sailing and steam-power cutters. The steamers with considerably shallower drafts were of a particular benefit along the Texas Gulf Coast and its inlets.

Since 1790, the longest-serving Coast Guard cutter in the Brazos Santiago Pass was the CGC *Point Nowell*, having served the area for thirty consecutive years, from 1967 to 1997. Master Chief Ambrose A. Pechacek was its first officer in charge, beginning in 1967. He was in attendance (thirty years later) as a retired Coast Guard member when the *Point Nowell* was decommissioned in 1997.

Today, the new marine protector class of cutters is patrolling the Brazos Santiago Pass, with a homeport at Station South Padre Island.

Sailing revenue cutters patrolled the Gulf of Mexico in the mid-1800s, during the war with Mexico, as far south as the Brazos Santiago Pass. *USCG Station SPI collection.*

Steamship revenue cutters also participated in the Brazos Santiago Pass, as their shallow draft proved very valuable for the pass and nearshore patrols. *USCG Station SPI collection.*

Above: The Coast Guard cutter *Point Nowell* at its South Padre Island moorings in 1967. It served for more than thirty years along the Texas border. *BMCM A. Pechacek's collection.*

Left: Master Chief Pechacek with his plank owner certificate. Plank owner status is a highly valued and respected position in the U.S. Coast Guard, honoring the original crew. *Author's collection.*

3

U.S. Life-Saving Service

1878-1915

T hrough the rallying efforts of private citizens and assisting those ensnared in the perils of the sea and maritime misfortune, the U.S. Life-Saving Service (USLSS) was created in 1878. Prior to this, in 1848, Congress approved the Newell Act to further what had previously been a volunteer search-and-rescue community. This put the responsibility of the life-saving service in the hands of the federal government. The United States Life-Saving Service was officially established as a service reporting to the United States Treasury Department.

The superintendent of the USLSS was Sumner I. Kimball, who was tasked with leading the effort to establish approximately 280 life-saving stations along the U.S. Eastern and Gulf Coast Shores. In Texas, 4 of those 280 were to be built; one in Galveston, another in Pass Cavallo, another in Mustang Island and the last in Brazos Santiago. The Station Brazos was assigned as Life-Saving Station No. 222.

STATION BRAZOS SANTIAGO (1881)

Brazos Island is the southernmost barrier island in Texas. It meets the Rio Grande River, the border between the United States and Mexico, to its south, and it meets the Brazos Santiago Pass, a natural water entrance leading to the Laguna Madre Bay, to its north. In modern times, the south jetty marks the northern point of Brazos Island.

Right: Sumner I. Kimball, the superintendent of the life-saving service from 1878 to 1915. He started his career as a clerk in the Treasury Department. *USCG Station SPI collection.*

Below: The United States of America flag flies proudly over the new Brazos Santiago Station, only a few miles from the Texas border. *LCDR C.R. Wilson's collection.*

In the 1800s, as a result of military influence, there was a thriving community on Brazos Island. In 1881, U.S. Life-Saving Station Brazos Santiago No. 222 was built on the northwestern side of Brazos Island.

Station Brazos Santiago was established on schedule, manned and considered to be in good working order. But as soon as it was completed, it was destroyed by a hurricane on August 12, 1880. What was left of the new building had to be taken down and rebuilt. Most of the outfitting and equipment were washed away at high tide and during the storm. Along with the life-saving station, the state quarantine station was also destroyed.

Almost a year and two weeks later, the U.S. Life-Saving Brazos Santiago Station was rebuilt, reoutfitted and considered ready for service once again. A search was put in place for a station keeper and crew. On December 31, 1881, Charles L. Cardiff was appointed as the first station keeper of the Brazos Santiago Station. The station remained in service for the next thirty-seven years.

Brazos Santiago Station Rescue logs (1883–1915)

The following log entries are from the Brazos Santiago Life-Saving Station and are maintained by the National Archives and Records Administration (NARA); Coast Guard Station South Padre Island houses the manuscripts. These entries by life-saving crewmembers give a glimpse into the day-to-day operations of being called into harm's way to assist ships and mariners along the coast of the Deep South.

Author's note: They have not been edited and are presented here, as they were written.

Jan 25–27, 1883, assisted the sloop Rescue, *carrying ballast. Persons on Board (POB): 5. Lives saved: N/A.*
At 8 o'clock in the evening on January 25, the crew of the Brazos station (eighth district), Texas, were on the outlook, when the heavy fog then prevailing fail away a little, and they saw a steamer and a sloop coming up toward the bar from the northeast. The fog soon closed in again and did not lift until 9 o'clock in the following morning (January 26), when the keeper discovered the sloop ashore on the southeast point of Padre Island, where she had grounded about an hour after the glimpse had of her the evening before. The surf boat was at once launched for the vessel, which was found to be the Rescue *of Corpus Christi, Texas, bound front that place in ballast two-point Isabel, Texas, with three passengers on board and a crew of two men. She was found lying in 3 feet of water and clear of the surf. The station crew road two-point Isabel to get the means for her release, and returning, worked on her all afternoon. The next morning (January 27), they again went out to her at 6 o'clock, and, it being found that she needed certain repairs, engaged in the effort to haul her on shore, assisted by the captain and five men from the schooner* Laura Lewis. *By 4 o'clock in the afternoon, they had her on the beach, 20 feet above high watermark. A few days afterward, she was floated and went on to her port.*

April 6, 1883, assisted the schooner William Whitehead, *carrying ballast POB: six Lives saved: six.*

At 9 o'clock in the morning the schooner William Whitehead *of New Orleans, Louisiana, with a crew of six men bound from Brazos Santiago, Texas, to Mobile, Alabama, in ballast, while standing out over Brazos Santiago Bar, on her way to sea, stranded on the north shoal or break or off the southeast point of Padre Island, about 3 miles northeast of the Brazos station (eighth district), on Brazos Island, coast of Texas. The accident was caused by the wind dying out, and the vessel losing steerage-way, was at once carried to the strong ebb-tide onto the shoal. She was observed to fetch up by the life-saving crew, and as the pilot in charge hoisted a signal of distress they went off as quickly as possible to her assistance. When they got on board, she was stomping quite hard and a portion of her false keel had been knocked off. Quick work was therefore necessary in order to float her off before she bilged. An anchor was accordingly run out with the surf-boat to a long scope of hawser, and after some hours of hard heaving, they succeeded in sluing the schooner's head to the sea, which was very rough. Fortunately, a fresh breeze sprang up from the northeast about the same time, and by setting the foresail and jibs, they forced her, as she lifted on the seas, over the bar and into deep water, where she was brought to anchor soon after 2:00 PM. She had sprung her rudder-head and was leaking, but as there were no facilities for repairing at Brazos, it was decided by the captain to proceed on his voyage, which he did a few days later, after making such temporary repairs to the rider as he was able. In this case, the life-saving crew no doubt aided very materially in saving the vessel from going to pieces on the shoal.*

December 7, 1883, assisted the steamer Morgan
Owing to light winds and flood tide, the pilot boat was unable to go outside. Launched surfboat and took the pilot out to her, sounding the channel over the bar on the way. Steamer was brought inside on the eighth instant.

April 5, 1884, a vessel carrying lard
A barrel of lard that was found on the beach was taken to station by crew and held there until the 20th, when it was forwarded to the owner, who had identified his property.

October 25, 1884, assisted the schooner Ada, *POB 3*
At about 6 o'clock in the morning, while the pilot-boat Ada *of Brazos de Santiago, Texas, carrying a crew of three men, was standing over*

the Brazos Bar, with the quarantine physician who wanted to board an incoming vessel, light baffling winds, together with the strong reflux of the tide, set her in the north breakers, where she stranded. The life-saving crew of the Brazos station (eighth district), coast of Texas, at once put off in the surfboat to the scene, a mild distant, and succeeded in getting the imperiled craft afloat and towing her out of danger. They then ran a line to the steamer Santiago, which took the vessel clear of the shoals. The surf man got back to their quarters at half past 10.

December 4, 1884, assisted the American schooner Frank Hitchcock
Three and quarter mile south of the station, the vessel aground. Informed the agent of the Rio Grande Railway Company of her situation, and, as she could not be floated, assisted wreckers in stripping her.

January 23, 1885, assisted the barge Hattie
In the bay. At 5 o'clock in the evening, the crew launched their boat in response to a signal for assistance and recovered a yawl which had broken a draft from the barge Hattie lying in the bay.

January 27, 1885, assisted American schooner Laura Lewis, carrying lumber, POB 5, Lives saved 5
The bar at Brazos de Santiago, Texas. At about 11 o'clock in the morning, the schooner Laura Lewis, of Brownsville, Texas, bound from Lake Charles, Louisiana, to her homeport with a cargo of lumber and having a crew of five men, struck bottom while crossing the bar at Brazos de Santiago, Texas. She quickly became unmanageable and drifted on the north breakers. Half an hour later, the keeper and crew of the Brazos station (eighth district) distant a mile and a half, had launched their surf-boat and arrived on board. And anger was ran out to the southward and a strain hove on the hawser, but all efforts of the crew to move her proving ineffectual, it was determined to throw the deck-load over-board in order to lighten her. This also failed, and as she was now leaking badly, an attempt was made to pump her out. Despite their efforts, however, to save the vessel, the pumps became choked with sand, and she rapidly filled with water. The men were, therefore, landed with their effects and taken to the station. Next morning (28th), both crews went off to the rack, unbent her sales and running-rigging, which, with the booms and gas, were safely landed on the rafts made from lumber taken from the cargo. At one in the afternoon, the sea be-came so rough that the men abandoned the vessel and came ashore. They were sheltered at the station for nine days. On

February 5, the schooner, being a complete rack, was sold at public auction. A portion of the cargo was saved

March 16, 1885, assisted the schooner Ada, *POB 3*
Brazos bar: three-quarters of a mile northeast of the Brazos Station. Shortly after noon, the pilot-schooner Ada *of Brazos de Santiago, Texas, with a crew of three men, in attempting to pass in over Brazos Bar, got becalmed and was swept ashore by the strong current, about three-quarters of a mile northeast of the Brazos station (eighth district), coast of Texas. The life-saving crew, at once, went to her assistance, and after a few hours work, succeeded in catching her off into the channel, when a breeze having sprung up, she proceeded into the bay, all right.*

April 8, 1885, assisted schooner Inez Huston, *carrying ballast, POB 5*
Three quarters of a mile to the northward and westward of the Brazos Station. At about 7 o'clock in the morning, the schooner Inez Huston *of Brashear, Louisiana, with a crew of five men, bound from Brazos de Santiago, Texas, to Pascagoula, Mississippi, in ballast, missed stays as she was going about while beating down the narrows on her way out towards Brazos Bar, and before her anchor could hold her, she drifted ashore on the flats, about three-quarters of a mile to the north word and westward of the Brazos station (eighth district), Brazos Island, Texas. The life-saving crew reached her half an hour later and, after running a stout hawser to the opposite side of the pass, made strenuous efforts to get her afloat. They had labored for a couple of hours when the hawser parted. Another Hawser was obtained from the pilot-boat lying near, and a fresh attempt made to get the vessel afloat, but with-out success, the seriously she had sprung no doubt adding to the difficulty of releasing her. In the afternoon, at about half-past one, another hawser was stretched across the past, and by keeping the pumps going and downright hard heaving for several hours longer, in which they had the assistance of the pilot-boat crew, the schooner was got of float at about half-past eight and safely anchored in the bay. As she stilly badly and there were no facilities for repairing aft Brazos. the captain engaged extra men to assist at the pumps, and on the second day afterwards, proceeded on his voyage, intending to put into Galveston en route for repairs.*

October 6, 1885, assisted a steamer at the bar
The north patrol of the Brazos Station (eighth district), coast of Texas, having the watch from 8 o'clock to midnight, observing a steamer standing

in towards the bar burned his Coston light to warn her of danger. Soon after seeing the signal, she came safely to an anchor off the shoals and waited for daylight before entering the harbor.

January 8, 1886, assisted a destitute sailor
On this date, a destitute sailor, barefooted and sorely in need of clothing, arrived at the Brazos station (eighth district), coast of Texas. The keeper attended to his wants and furnished him with a pair of shoes from the supplies donated by the women's national relief association. The man was very grateful for the kindness shown him.

March 8, 1886, assisted the vessel Latta Mayo, *carrying bones, POB 3*
In the morning of this date, the schooner Latta Mayo of Brashear, Louisiana, left point Isabel, Texas, bound for Galveston in the same state, with a cargo of bones and a crew of three men. While trying to work out over the Brazos bar, against a light southeast breeze, she misstayed, and the tide set her on the southern point of Padre Island. The crew of the Brazos station (eighth district), coast of Texas, pulled off to the stranded vessel, laid out an anchor, and succeeded, after two hours of vigorous work, in heaving her afloat. She was then taken to a safe anchorage of breast of the lighthouse, having sustained no material damage.

March 11, 1886 assisted the schooner Phoenix *with a cargo of lumber, POB 4, Lives saved 4*
The lumber-laden schooner Phoenix of Lake Charles, Louisiana, bound thence to Brazos de Santiago, Texas, arrived off Brazos Pass about 9 o'clock in the morning of this date and signaled for a pilot. A violent southeast wind prevailed at the time and a high sea was running, which, together with the strong set of the flood tide, made it impossible for a pilot to go out over the bar. The range flags were hoisted to guide the schooner inside, and at half-past one, she squared away for the bar. The vessel struck bottom coming in, became unmanageable, and the northerly current and heavy breakers drove her ashore on the southeast point of Padre Island, where she bilged. The craft lay a mile northeast of the Brazos station (eighth district), coast of Texas, with a tremendous surf sweeping clean over her. The life-saving force launched their boat and immediately put off to the scene. After considerable difficulty, the crew of four men were taken from the rack and safely landed, the surfboat, which was all the while shipping water, being free by constant bailing. The vessel straightway commands to go to pieces,

much of her bottom planking being found washed up on the beach. The castaways were conducted to the station and furnished with a warm supper, and two of them were provided with dry clothing from the stock donated by the women's national relief association. They were fed and sheltered for three days. The two succeeding days (12th and 13th) the surfboat and attempted to board the schooner, but were prevented by the heavy weather, which continued unabated. On the 14th, what was left of the craft was sold by the captain, and she went into the hands of wreckers, who stripped her and saved a portion of the cargo. The following letter, expressing the gratitude of the master for the services rendered by the station crew, was subsequently received by the keeper: "POINT ISABEL, TEXAS, March 16, 1886. Yours, truly, DEAR. Sir: I am very much obliged for the kind services I have received from you and your crew and your assistance in trying to save the Schooner Phoenix. I am sincerely grateful to you all for saving our lives, and thankful for your kind treatment of me and my crew while at the station. A.F. DOBBERTIN, Master of schooner Phoenix, of Lake Charles, Louisiana. T.W. NORMAN, Captain of life-saving station at Brazos Santiago."

June 21, 1886, assisted the schooner Willie Ann

In the afternoon of this date, the schooner Willie Ann of Brashear, Louisiana, arrived off the bar near the Brazos station (eighth district), coast of Texas, and, wishing to enter the past, set a flag for a pilot. Some of the pilots being sick and the others absent at the time, the keeper was requested to hoist the range signals, which he did. The vessel, still remaining outside, and the weather threatening, the keeper went off and brought her in at the captain's risk, and anchored her safely at the quarantines station.

November 27, 1886, assisted a gunboat

In the afternoon of this date, the keeper of the Brazos station (eighth district), coast of Texas, at the request of the commander of a Mexican gunboat, loaned the station supply boat to transport a Hawser from Point Isabel to Brazos. The captain expressed his appreciation of the assistance rendered him in a letter to the keeper, of which the following is a translation: "Abelardo Pinto, commander of the Mexican gun-boat of war 20 Colon, certifies that, with one of the boats of the life-saving station of the United States of America, he transported from Point Isabel to the station at Brazos a manila cable weighing 528 pounds: 'in the name of my government I wish to express to you my sincere thanks.'—ABELARDO PINTO."

December 31, 1886 assisted a boat on the inner bay, POB 2, Lives saved 2
During a Norther, in the afternoon of this date, two men whose boat had capsized in the inner bay were provided by the serviceman of the Brazos station (eighth district), coast of Texas, with dry clothing from the supplies donated by the women's national relief association and were fed and sheltered two days.

January 2, 1887, assisted the steamer Aransas, *carrying general merchandise, POB 40, Lives saved 40*
Three-quarters of a mile northeast of the Brazos station, at 5 o'clock in the evening on January 2nd, sheetrock bottom, lost steerage way, and brought up on what are known as the south breakers, three-quarters of a mile to the northeastward of the Brazos station (eighth district). She was bound and to Brazos de Santiago, from Galveston, with a valuable cargo of general merchandise, and carrying a crew of 20–9 persons, besides 11 passengers, the district Superintendent being among the number. The life-saving crew had just got the surfboat ready for the purpose of taking off the laughter as soon as the steamer was safely in the harbor, but when they observed the accident no time was lost in reaching the scene. They help to put a large anchor on a pilot boat that had gone alongside, and this, with a hawser, subsequently hauled taut, was carried windward into deep water. Darkness now coming on, it was decided to suspend farther operations until morning. By direction of the superintendent, the serviceman remained on the vessel, so as to be at hand in case of emergency and to render to the ship's company any aid that might be necessary. The wind blew pretty strong during the night, making up a rough sea, and at 3 o'clock in the morning, the hawser parted, causing the steamer to work farther southward on the shoal. The starboard anchor was let go, which held her for about an hour, when a heavy surge snapped the cable, and she swung hand toward the beach. A pilot boat was now dispatched to Point Isabel for an anchor and lines, but did not return until late in the evening, when it was too dark to resume work. The life-saving crew, however, still continued on board. At about midnight (3rd) the vessel, which had all along been lying in an easy position, began to pound heavily, the sea having perceptibly increased, and at daylight (4th) the passengers, consisting of six men, three women, and a child, becoming alarmed for their safety, were landed in the surfboat on Brazos Island Beach, two trips through the breakers being necessary for that purpose. The entire day, the station man assisted in running anchors and hawsers, and in the evening, before returning to their quarters, ran a short

line, as a matter of precaution, from the steamer to the shore. From this time on to the 13th, the serviceman were in constant attendance, actively pushing the work preparatory to floating the vessel, and carrying dispatches to and fro, averaging nearly 5 trips a day in their boat. After unloading two-thirds of her cargo, she was finally gotten clear on the last-mentioned date and taken inside, having sustained considerable damage to the hull. The next day, she proceeded to New Orleans, under convoy, for repairs. The annexed letter was received by the keeper from the agent of the steam-ship line. "SOUTHERN PACIFIC COMPANY, BRAZOS DE SANTIAGO, January 14, 1887. MY DEAR SIR : Before leaving this harbor, I beg to return the thanks of the company I represent, as well as my own, for the efficient service rendered the steamship Aransas by yourself and the boats crew during the last 10 days that the ship has been stranded among the breakers of Brazos Bar. And I desire to say that launching boats through the surf, running lines, etc., In such waters as has been experienced during this time, are not only unpleasant but dangerous. I repeat my thanks for your prompt action on this occasion and of which I shall take pleasure in communicating at an early day to the general manager of this company. I remain, yours, very truly, CHARLES FARLEY, Agent Southern Pacific Company. Captain NORMAN, life-saving service at Brazos Island." A few weeks later, the steamship line, through its agent, in recognition of the valuable service rendered on this occasion, presented the lifesaving crew was several hundred dollars.

December 11, 1887, assisted the steamer Aransas, carrying general merchandise, POB 36, Lives saved 36
At half-past 1 o'clock in the afternoon, the steamer Aransas of New Orleans, Louisiana, dragged her anchor in Brazos Santiago Bay, coast of Texas, and grounded on the middle shoal, a mile north of the Brazos station (eighth district). The keeper and two of his crew manned a skiff and ran a line from the vessel to the steam-lighter Santiago, which then succeeded in pulling the craft afloat. Early in the morning of the 13th, the Aransas, detained in port by a north-west gale of wind, again dragged from her anchorage and went ashore on the north point of Brazos Island. The life-saving crew went off to her in the surfboat, and, at the captain's request, pulled to Point Isabel, 3 miles distant, for a tug, but by the time they returned, the action on the blood-tide had enabled the steamer to work herself clear without assistance. She was bound to Corpus Christi, Texas, with a general cargo, and had onboard seven passengers in a crew numbering twenty-nine.

December 13, 1887, assisted the steamer Aransas, *carrying general merchandise*
Point of Brazos Island. Casualty: vessel, cargo or life: Unidentified

April 27th, 1888, assisted the steamer Aransas
During the day, the steamer Aransas *of New Orleans, Louisiana, arrived of breast of the Brazos station (eighth district), coast of Texas, with her shaft broken and propeller gone. She signaled the keeper to telegraph the news to an agent of the vessel, which he promptly did. She required no other assistance from the life-savers.*

February 27, 1891, assisted the schooner Ada
Three-quarters of a mile north-northeast of station. Misstayed and went ashore in the breakers. Ran anchor and enable the vessel to get off without damage.

November 9, 1891, assisted a skiff at the beach
Drifted onto the beach. Hauled it up clear and secured it for the owner.

January 2, 1892, assisted a boat adrift
Overhauled and took it to a secure place.

January 21, 1892, assisted a steamer
Shortly before midnight, the watchman saw the lights of the steamer approaching the bar. His warning signal was immediately flashed, whereupon the vessel stood offshore.

August 27, 1895, assisted the schooner Ada
Three quarters of a mile north of station. Casualty: vessel, cargo or life: unidentified.

August 29, 1895, assisted persons in distress
Transported 11 people from partially submerged island to small schooner, in which they were taken to place of safety.

August 29, 1895, assisted schooner A.J. Perkins *with a cargo of lumber*
Seven miles southeast of station. Stranded; foresail lost for rigging damaged, and yawl carried away; center-board jammed. Station crews ran anchors and endeavored to float her; also renewed the effort on the following day, on

August 31, assisted to lighten cargo of lumber. On September 4, floated her to safety.

December 4, 1895, assisted the schooner James Anderson
Five-eighths east-northeast of station. Casualty: vessel, cargo or life: unidentified.

February 27, 1896, assisted the British steamer Maristow
Seven miles southeast of station. At daylight, a boat belonging to this steamer was cited making for the beach some distance from station. Surfboat was launched and crew pulled to Padre point, where boat had landed. Learned that the steamer had broken her shaft about 400 miles north of Veracruz. Mate, with boats crew, left her on the 21ˢᵗ to find telegraphic communication. Station crew assisted in launching ship's boat and directed the mate to nearest telegraph station. On morning of March 1, the steamer was sighted, 7 miles southeast of station, flying distress signals. Manned surf-boat and pulled down to her. Told master that his boat's crew had landed safely and telegraphed for assistance. Steamer was brought to anchor, and master was landed in surfboats to communicate with agents. On March 4, she was taken in tow for Galveston and reach there safely.

January 22, 1898, assisted the schooner Marie Isabel
In attempting the bar without a pilot the schooner struck, but succeeded in working off and stood away about 3 miles, when she hove to and set a signal of distress. The surf and boarded her and found her leaking and her steering gear disabled; recent sale, repaired steering gear, and beat up to the bar, where she was turned over to pilot. Two of the crew remained by to pump until the schooner was well inside.

May 20, 1898, assisted the steamer Clinton
Entrance to the harbor. Stranded in the north breakers at the entrance to the harbor and set distress signal. Surf month boarded her and landed the purser to go for assistance, then returned and took ashore the two passengers and carried a message to the vessel's agents. The agents and purser made arrangements with lighters and wired to Galveston for a tug, which arrived on the 24ᵗʰ. From the 20ᵗʰ to the 28ᵗʰ, on which day the vessel was floated, the station crew rendered assistance in carrying messages between ship and shore, running lines to lighters and the tug, helping to plant anchors to heave the vessel off, and doing general boat duty in the interest of the master and

the wrecking company. The vessel was but slightly damaged, and after minor repairs, proceeded on her route.

May 21, 1899, assisted the schooner Olga
Three quarters of a mile northeast of the station. Stranded on the shawl, surf men boarded her, laid out an anchor and hove a strain on the hawser. As the tide came in, the vessel was gradually worked afloat without sustaining any damage.

May 18, 1900, assisted a sloop carrying ballast
One half mile north of station. Capsized in a strong southeast wind about ½ mile north of station. The sloop, being heavily ballasted, sank at once in about 8 feet of water, leaving the occupants (four boys) clinging to the mast and rigging. Surf men rescued the boys, one of whom was much exhausted, and subsequently, they raised and bailed out the sloop.

March 21, 1901, assisted the schooner C.H. Moore
One mile northwest of the station. Stranded on the middleground about 1 mile northwest of station. Surf ran her hawer to an old wharf on the island and then assisted to heave taut on the windlass. At high water, she floated without injury and proceeded to see.

May 5, 1901, assisted steamer Olga
Southeast end of Padre Island/1 mile north, ½ mile east of station. Having missed stays, this vessel was carried by the strong ebb tide into the breakers on the southeast end of Padre Island. Surf month went on board and endeavored to run out a small anchor but could not do so on account of the strong current. They stood by until the tide slackened, and then planted the anchor. As the tide flooded, they slowly worked her into the channel, and about 5 AM, they succeeded in sailing her into the harbor without damage to vessel or cargo.

July 13, 1901, assisted persons
Sixteen persons who were forced to leave their home by the unusual high water were succored at the lifesaving station on the 13th and 14th instants.

August 4, 1902, funeral arrangements
At 1:45 PM, the station keeper went to Point Isabel, upon request, and ordered a coffin for the keeper of the Brazos Santiago Lighthouse, who had died suddenly, and after returning, detailed a surf man to care for the

light-house during the absence of the assistant light keeper, who was the son of the deceased, and consequently desirous of attending the funeral. On the following day, the station keeper went to Point Isabel in supply boat and transported assistant light keeper and family to the lighthouse.

October 5, 1902, assisted a schooner
Near the bar. At 11:10 PM, the north patrol cited a schooner standing dangerously near the bar and warn her off with a Coston light.

February 16, 1903, assisted the schooner Pierce Simpson, *carrying a cargo of rice*
Three quarters of a mile west and ½ miles south of station. Drag anchor during a strong wind and grounded on the flats three quarters of a mile from station, at 1 AM, ran out anchors and shove her off a short distance, but she grounded on the following tide and was finally floated only after lightning her cargo of rice.

March 1, 1903, assisted the schooner Manteao, *POB 2, Lives saved 2*
Off the bar. Carried away main boom and a strong wind and anchored off the bar at 11:40 AM, soon afterwards, the steamer Manteo, *and anchor nearby, signaled "send a boat" and despite high surf along the beach, the station crew succeeded in launching the surfboat, and pulled to the schooner. She was riding in apparent security at her anchors, with no one on board, and, finding that her crew of two was aboard the* Manteo, *the life-savers started back for their station. They had a hard struggle, but all reached sure in safety. After the weather moderated, the crew of the schooner repaired her broken boom, and surf man boarded, and assisted to get her underway and work her to the bar, when the master took her into port.*

April 15, 1903, assisted the schooner Pierce Simpson
On the bar. Grounded on the bar while trying to make the harbor. Station crew ran her anchor and hove her afloat, when she slipped her cable and proceeded into port, the surf men later recovering the anchor.

May 23, 1903, assisted a skiff in the harbor
In response to a signal from the steamer Manteo, *the life-saving crew pulled out and surfboat, picked up a pilot who had left the steamer in a small skiff, landed him through the surf, and assisted him to get his skiff through the breakers and haul it up on the shore.*

August 14, 1903, assisted the schooner Olga *with POB three*
Near Padre Island. Set a signal calling for the life-saving crew to come to her assistance. The master then lowered a boat manned by the mate and to semen, intending to run an anchor, but the boat capsized in the breakers, and its crew, fortunately, succeeded in landing safely on Padre Island. Meanwhile, the surfboat left the station shorthanded and pulled to the pilot boat Ada, *where three volunteers were secured then picked up the mate from Padre Island, and pulled to the stranded craft. The vessel, however, had shifted position so that she afforded no lee for the life-savers, who found it impossible to get alongside through the seething mass of breakers, and as she appeared to lie easy and was in no immediate danger of breaking up, it was decided to abandon operations until a more favorable time. The next day, the wind and sea had moderated, and the surf man rendered assistance by caring dispatches, running lines, and performing other necessary duty until the 19ᵗʰ, when they boarded the schooner* Olga *and help to lay out a heavy anchor from the stranded vessel to deep water outside the bar. At 10 PM, the* Manteo *was floated, and the next morning, she went into the harbor, having sustained no major injury.*

October 16, 1903, assisted the schooner Josephine D., *carrying a cargo of break, POB 2, lives saved 2*
Brazos Island, ¼ mile northeast of station. Missed stays in a light breeze with strong tide and stranded on the shore of Brazos Island, 1 mile northeast of station. The life-saving crew assisted in removing about 5 tons of freight from the vessel, but, owing to high surf, was unable to get her afloat until the 19ᵗʰ, when they ran an anchor offshore hove the schooner off the beach, and assisted her crew to make sale. As the schooner was but a small craft, her crew of two were provided with food in quarters at the station while she lay ashore.

November 2, 1903, assisted a sailboat, POB 2, lives saved 2
Capsized; two occupants being picked up by a near-by rowboat. Four surf men in station supply boat righted the sailboat, towed it to Isabel, and delivered it to owner.

November 26, 1903, assisted the schooner Josephine D., *with a cargo of tile pipe*
On the beach. Stranded on the beach while attempting to enter the harbor; the life-saving crew waded out to her, carried ashore two women passengers,

and took them to the station. The life-savers then assisted to unload the cargo of tile pipe, piling it on the beach, take ashore the personal effects of passengers and crew, and afterwards to strip the vessel.

February 12, 1904, assisted a yawl belonging to the vessel Ada
Yawl, no name, and a pilot and boatman were on their way to when their yawl capsized on the bar a mile from the station. The life-savers had already harnessed their team in anticipation of the accident, as the sea was running high, and they immediately hauled the surfboat to the beach and pulled to the imperiled men, who were clinging to the overturned boat, rescued them, and took them out to the Hughes. Finding that the tug drew too much water to cross the bar in safety, the surfmen took her passengers, three in number, to a pilot boat at anchor inside, then pulled to the capsized yawl and towed it to the pilot boat.

March 10, 1904, assisted the schooner Lehman No. 3
In the harbor. Stranded while endeavoring to beat out the harbor and, in response to a signal of distress, the life-saving crew ran out an anchor and assisted to heave the vessel into deep water.

March 10, 1904, assisted the schooner Lehman No. 3
Seven-eighths of a mile northwest of station. Unidentified assistance.

March 10, 1904, assisted the schooner Lehman No. 3
Mile west by north of the station. Parted anchor chain and stranded of about mile west by north of the station; the life-savers went on board her, obtain an anchor from a pilot boat, planted it, ran a line to the schooner, dragged for and found the anchor, which had been lost, and then made an unsuccessful attempt to pump her out, and then assisted to transfer the cargo of lumber to a lighter. On the 27th instant, the schooner was stripped and abandoned.

January 28, 1907, assisted a catboat
Parted cable and drifting to sea before northwest gale. Discovered by patrol at 4:50 AM, he secured the boat and notified keeper. The life-savers proceeded to her and hauled her up on the beach.

August 21, 1908, assisted the launch Joe
Discovered by keeper at 7:15 PM, 1 mile north of the station, with disabled engine and in danger of being carried out of the pass by the strong ebb tide.

October 23, 1908, assisted the sloop Aldrine
Adrift 1 mile west of the station. Picked up by surfmen and taken to a safe anchorage.

October 27, 1908, assisted the schooner Jeff N. Miller
Parted its chain and drifted down the channel mile west northwest of the station. Life-savers got aligned to her from a war and swaddle her alongside.

November 3, 1908, assisted the schooner Jeff N. Miller
Three-quarters of a mile west-northwest of station. Pounding on the bottom while lying at anchor ¾ mile west northwest of station, none of her crew being aboard. Surfmen went aboard, weighed anchor, set sail, and work the schooner to a safe berth.

November 10, 1908, assisted the schooner Jeff N. Miller
Three-quarters of a mile west northwest of station. Anchor and chain loss by schooner October 27.

December 2, 1908, assisted the launch Sea Gull, *POB 12, lives saved 12*
Lost in the fog and stranded three-quarters mile northwest of the station, with 12 persons aboard. Discovered by the keeper, and the surfboat was sent to their aid. Passengers were taken off while the life-savers floated the launch, and were then returned aboard. Keeper piloted the Sea Gull *to Isabel.*

December 3, 1908, assisted the schooner Jeff N. Miller
Three-quarter mile west-northwest of station. Unidentified assistance.

March 15, 1909, assisted a skiff
A fisherman reported to the keeper that his boat, containing three valuable seines, had been cut adrift. Surfmen made a thorough search along the beach and discovered this gift to mile south of the station. Brought to the station and restored to owner. The seines were not found.

May 9, 1909, assisted the sloop Esperanza
Unidentified assistance.

May 17, 1909, assisted a sloop
Broke rudder gudgeon and was beached near station. Surfmen assisted to repair the broken gudgeon and float her.

May 19, 1909, public assistance
A man with a badly crushed hand; injury dressed.

May 19, 1909, assisted the launch Sea Gull, *POB 11, lives saved 11*
Two and one-half miles northwest of station. Engine broke down. Signaled
for assistance. Life-saving crew responded in surfboat and towed her to
Point Isabel. The 11 passengers were anxious to catch the afternoon train
and were very appreciative of the service.

August 1, 1914, assisted the motorboat Monarch, *POB five*
Piloted motorboat over bar and into harbor.

August 23, 1914, assisted the schooner Emily P. Wright *with a cargo of*
ammunition, POB 11, lives saved 10
Wrecked on Mexican coast 140 miles south; crew picked up along coast in
famished condition; take into station and given food, etc.

LIFE-SAVING SERVICE: SAVES
OUR LADY OF THE SEA STATUE (1884)

Surfman Enarnacion Delgado was walking the beach on South Padre Island, very likely on patrol, when he spotted something glistening in the sunlight. On further inspection and after digging it out with his bare hands, he found an eighteen-inch-tall statue of Mother Mary and her baby, the Christ child, Jesus. Delgado cleaned it up and presented it to the Our Lady Star of the Sea Church in Port Isabel. It has survived hurricanes, storms and fires that the church buildings that have housed it did not. Its origin is unknown, but the local citizens regard it as a gift from the sea—a blessing.

It is considered a symbol of blessing by many in the area. The found statue is highly coveted by the citizens of the maritime community. *Author's collection.*

CHIEF WARRANT OFFICER WALLACE L. REED (1905)

The present-day Coast Guard Station South Padre Island is located at the end of Wallace Reed Road. The road is named in honor of Chief Warrant Officer (CWO) Reed. He served as the officer in charge/station keeper at Life-Saving Station No. 222, then at the temporary station at Brazos Santiago Lighthouse and, lastly, at the Coast Guard Lifeboat Station Point Isabel (located on South Padre Island, built in 1923). He was responsible for the rescue station for twenty-seven years.

CWO Wallace L. Reed was the longest-serving station keeper/officer-in-charge. He served for nearly three decades in both the life-saving service and Coast Guard. *USCG Station SPI collection.*

CWO Reed was born on January 24, 1874, in Camden, New Jersey, the son of a ship captain who owned his own boat. In 1900, he joined the U.S. Life-Saving Service and was sent to Galveston, Texas. He arrived in time for the 1900 hurricane, when the life-saving station and most of Galveston Island were destroyed. He served in Texas and Florida for a few years, and on Christmas Eve in 1905, he reported to the Point Isabel area and assumed command of the life-saving station on Brazos Island.

In 1919, under his leadership, the rescue team responded to the distressed schooner *Cape Horn* and its crew of eight sailors on September 16, 1919. The vessel had been caught in a storm that was recognized as one of the worst storms in the history of the Gulf of Mexico. It was known as the Florida Keys Hurricane of 1919. The rescue team consisted of the officer in charge, Wallace Reed; a boatswain's mate, first-class, Pablo Valent; and Surfmen Mariano Holland, Indalecio Lopez and three others, for a rescue crew of seven.

In spotting the distressed schooner, a surf boat was launched from the beach, and in an effort to row over the bar, it encountered unusually high crashing waves and the worst conditions to date. After battling the seas for more than two hours, the surf boat came along the leeward side and in close quarters of the *Cape Horn* and quickly assessed the situation as being dire. Reed decided to remove the eight stranded sailors, one at a time, requiring excellent and precise coxswain commands to row the rescue boat with the timing of the crashing waves for eight individual attempts. All eight sailors

The Silver Life-Saving Medal has been issued since 1874 and is awarded for rescuing drowning or shipwrecked persons. *USCG Station SPI collection.*

were brought on board the Coast Guard rescue boat for a total of fifteen persons on board. While the sailors had been rescued, they and the rescue team were not out of harm's way, as they then had to row their way back across the bar and through treacherous breaking waves. In an effort to keep the rescue boat from being tossed to the point of capsizing, Coxswain Reed directed his crew to deploy a sea drogue. A sea drogue is a bucket-like device that is tethered off the back of the boat in an effort to slow down the force of waves to keep the vessel upright and maneuverable. The seas were very demanding, and the drogue eventually failed at a critical point, but the boat, crew and survivors all made it safely to land, though wet and exhausted.

The Coast Guard rescue team received the highly coveted Silver Life-Saving Medal for unusual heroism in rescuing the crew of the schooner *Cape Horn*. The Life-Saving Medal is rare among U.S. medals. It is made from the eponymous precious metal silver and has an economic value, and each medal issued bears the recipient's name, which is inscribed on the back.

4
U.S. Coast Guard
1915-Present

In 1915, Captain Ellsworth Price Bertholf of the U.S. Revenue Cutter Service was appointed by the Treasury Department as commandant of the newly formed Coast Guard, a result of combining the life-saving service and the revenue cutter service into one department: the United States Coast Guard.

World War I efforts required a more focused effort on military operations, with the newly formed Coast Guard patrolling and protecting America's shores and harbors while also supporting naval operations in Europe. In times of war, the Coast Guard has a rich and long history of being moved from its parent department (Treasury, Transportation, Homeland Security, etc.) to lend its expertise to the U.S. Navy and Department of Defense in times of crisis. Coast Guard Station Brazos Santiago played an essential role in patrolling the southernmost beaches of the United States during World War I, as did Coast Guard Station Point Isabel during World War II.

Today, the Coast Guard is forty-two thousand strong, with assets all over the United States and points of interest around the world. Coast Guard Station South Padre Island has taken over the "watch" and responsibilities from the now-historic Coast Guard Station Point Isabel, which took over the "watch" and responsibilities from Coast Guard/Life-Saving Station Brazos Santiago.

COAST GUARD STATION BRAZOS SANTIAGO: RESCUE LOGS (1915–1923)

The following log entries are from the Brazos Santiago Life-Saving Station are maintained by the National Archives and Records Administration (NARA), and Coast Guard Station South Padre Island houses the manuscripts. These entries by life-saving crewmembers give a glimpse into the day-to-day operations of being called into harm's way to assist ships and mariners along the coast of the Deep South.

Author's note: these entries have not been edited and are presented here as they were written.

> *January 16, 1915, assisted the schooner* Corpus Christi, *POB five*
> *Leaking in heavy seas; piloted through difficult channel to safe harbor.*

> *February 7, 1915, assisted the motorboat* Martha J., *POB two*
> *Floated stranded motorboat.*

> *March 13, 1915, assisted the motorboat* Martha J. *with a cargo of divers' gear, POB four*
> *Towed disabled motorboat into harbor.*

> *July 16, 1915, assisted the motorboat* Martha J. *with a cargo of salvaging gear and provisions, POB eight*
> *Lost propeller, helpless; towed to port.*

> *August 1, 1915, assisted the skiff* Bath, *POB three, lives saved three*
> *Brazos de Santiago bar. Capsized in surf; men clinging to the boat; picked up and taken to station.*

> *March 13, 1916, assisted the motorboat* Martha J., *POB one*
> *Off station. Engine disabled; towed to port.*

> *May 14, 1916, assisted the motorboat* Julia B., *POB 35*
> *Laguna moderate. Engine disabled; towed to a wharf.*

> *August 13, 1916, assisted motorboat* Julia B., *POB two*
> *One and a half miles northwest. Engine disabled; towed to point Isabel, Texas.*

August 18, 1916, assisted motorboat Julia B.
Three and a half miles west. Beached to prevent destruction and hurricane.

August 18, 1916, assisted the motorboat Ada
Three and a half miles west. Beached to prevent destruction and hurricane.

August 18, 1916, assisted the sloop San Juan
Three and a half miles west. Beached to prevent destruction and hurricane.

August 18, 1916, assisted the sloop Kingfisher
Three and a half miles west. Beached to prevent destruction and hurricane.

August 18, 1916, assisted the sloop Tamaulipas
Three and a half miles west. Beached to prevent destruction and hurricane.

August 18, 1916, assisted personnel, lives saved 22
Took 12 men, one woman, and nine children off Padre Island *and carried them to Point Isabel for safety from hurricane.*

October 8, 1916, assisted the motorboat Ada, *POB eight, lives saved 8*
2 miles northwest. Capsized and sunk; rescued occupants and raised in bailed out boat.

October 22 and 23ʳᵈ, 1916, assisted sloop Baby, *POB 4, life saved 4*
Four miles northwest. Capsized in rough sea; rescued crew, righted boat, and towed it to port is about Texas.

January 20, 1917, assisted the motorboat Gladys *with a cargo of mail, POB 4*
One mile north. Stranded in fog; ran anchor, hove boat off, and piloted her to a wharf.

July 8, 1917, assisted the sloop Caxaca, *POB 14, Lives saved 14*
One and a half miles northwest. Dismasted in race, in danger of filling; cleared away the wreckage and towed boat to Point Isabel.

July 14, 1917, assisted the motorboat Julia B., *POB 29*
One and a half miles northwest. Stranded, took off some of the passengers and pulled boat afloat, then sent party on their way.

July 16, 1917, assisted soldier
One and a half miles north. Soldier bather rescues by his comrades, underwater 10 to 15 minutes; resuscitated by station crew after nearly 3 hours work.

July 27, 1917, assisted people on island
Four miles north. Carried from Padre Island to Port Isabel, Tex. Seven men endangered by high tide and sea.

October 29, 1917, assisted the sloop Lone Star, *POB three, lives saved three*
Four and a half miles northwest. Leaking badly in storm; took off occupants, and conveyed them and boat to Port Isabel, Tex.

January 7, 1918, assisted the motorboat Charlotte, *POB 18*
One and a half miles northwest. Engine disabled; picked up and towed to Port Isabel.

February 24, 1918, assisted the motorboat Charlotte, *POB 14*
Two miles northwest. Engine disabled; towed to Point Isabel and landed 12 passengers.

April 14, 1918, assisted a skiff, POB one, life saved one
One mile north-northwest. Occupants fell overboard while making landing; rescued from alongside boat.

January 23, 1919, assisted the motorboat industry, POB five
One mile west. Unacquainted with channel; pulled afloat and taken to safe anchorage.

May 8, 1919, assisted the sloop Zu Zu, *POB two*
One mile west. Lost sale in storm; picked up and towed to Padre Island.

September 13, 1919, assisted 29 people from island
Took off Padre Island and carried to point Isabel 29 persons seeking safety from approaching storm.

September 16, 1919, assisted the schooner Cape Horn *with a cargo of fish and ice, POB eight, lives saved*

Eight miles east. Vessel rendered a derelict in hurricane; but offshore in high seas and rescued crew under circumstances of extreme hazard; commanded by headquarters

December 16, 1919, assisted the motorboat Grazia Cerino *with a cargo of ice, POB five*
Piloted out over bar to sea.

December 22, 1919 assisted motorboat Spectre *with a cargo of fish, POB 5*
Engine disabled outside harbor; towed safely in.

December 28, 1919, assisted motorboat Spectre *with a cargo of fish, POB 6*
Quarter of a mile north. Stranded; work afloat and sent on way.

January 18, 1920, assisted motorboat Julia B., *POB 14*
One mile north northwest. Fuel loss through leak; put 10 gallons on board.

January 20, 1920, assisted a sloop
Four miles northwest. Ran on snag; unable to get clear; freed and towed to Point Isabel.

February 20, 1920, assisted the motorboat Spectre *with a cargo of fish, POB 8*
One and a half miles west. Ran out of channel and stranded; work afloat by use of sales and engine.

April 6, 1920, assisted motorboat Charlotte, *POB nine*
One mile northwest. Stranded in rough sea; landed seven persons; floated vessel and supplied her with gasoline.

June 3, 1920, assisted the barge Tennessee Girl *with a cargo of petroleum, POB three*
Three miles east. Lying at anchor; waterlogged; got anchors and towed vessel to port.

September 3, 1920, assisted the sloop Nene, *carrying a cargo of fishing nets, POB two*

Six miles north. Anchored; unable to proceed on account of light when an adverse current; towed to harbor.

December 23, 1920, assisted the motorboats Hohea, Toltica, *and* Melloise, *POB 17*
Two miles north. Endangered in high seas; brought into harbor and safely anchored.

December 28, 1920, assisted the Mexican motorboat Olympia, *POB six*
At station. Unfamiliar with local water; piloted boat over bar.

December 30, 1920, assisted the Mexican motorboats Nohea, Toltica, *and* Melloise, *POB 17*
At station. In harbor, afraid to proceed on account of high seas and heavy weather, piloted two outer bar; vessel then headed for Tampico.

January 1, 1921, assisted the motorboat Charlotte, *POB one person*
One hundred yards north. Ran on submerged snag, while making landing, and stove a large hole in port bow; hold port bow out of water, made temporary repairs and launched boat.

January 10, 1921, assisted motorboat Olympia *with a cargo of ice, POB six*
Five hundred yards north. Unfamiliar with channel; stranded; floated in piloted over bar.

January 16, 1921, assisted the motorboat Olympia, *carrying a cargo of fish, POB 6*
One mile northeast. Unfamiliar with channel; piloted into harbor; next day, searched vessel, after which allowed her to proceed.

March 7, 1921, assisted Mexican motorboat Olympia *with a cargo of fish, POB five ·*
One mile northeast. Piloted vessel in over bar, she being afraid to come in alone.

May 13, 1921, assisted motorboat Yvonne, *POB 2*
One mile northeast, piloted vessel into harbor.

May 29, 1921, assisted motorboat Yvonne, *POB 5*
One half mile west. Unfamiliar with channel; stranded; after much effort bloated boat, then towed it to Point Isabel; landed passengers and crew.

May 14 and 15th, 1921, assisted the motorboat Sunflower II, *POB three*
One mile northeast. Piloted vessel into harbor; next day, piloted her out over bar.

June 2, 1921, assisted a skiff, POB 2, life saved 2
A quarter of a mile northeast. Unable to make headway against strong current; picked up and towed into harbor.

June 5, 1921, assisted with a drowning victim
Eight hundred yards northeast. Recovered from water an apparently drowned man; after employing resuscitating treatment for 30 minutes, restored man to consciousness; then took him to station, furnished him with dry clothing and later transported him to point Isabel, Tex.

Coast Guard Station Brazos Santiago
(1919–1923)

In 1918, a new Coast Guard Brazos Santiago Station was being built on wood pilings on the north end of Brazos Island to protect it from storm surges. Sadly, only a few months after the station was complete, on September 14, 1919, it was in the direct path of the Florida Keys Hurricane, considered the worst in Texas history. As the storm swept across Texas, it all but completely wiped out the new 1919 Coast Guard station.

The crew of Coast Guard Station Brazos Santiago are in dress white uniforms, proudly displaying the larger "holiday flag" of the United States of America. *LCDR C.R. Wilson's collection.*

Station Keeper Wallace L. Reed and his crew relocated to the Brazos Santiago Lighthouse and shared the space with the lighthouse keeper and continued station operations. Wallace was the last station keeper of Life-Saving Station Brazos Santiago. The station crew operated out of the lighthouse for the next four years until 1923, when a new Coast Guard Point Isabel Station was built on the south end of South Padre Island (across the pass from the former Brazo Santiago station). In 1958, the station land on Brazos Island was transferred to the Brownsville Navigation District.

Law Enforcement and the Volstead Act (1919)

In 1919, the National Prohibition Act went into effect, prohibiting the transportation of alcohol into the United States. This required the newly formed Coast Guard Station Brazos Santiago to begin patrolling to keep illegal alcohol from making its way into Texas and crossing the border at the mouth of the Rio Grande River (the station's southern border), where it meets the Gulf of Mexico. The station is located a mere six nautical miles north of the United States–Mexico border, where illegal border crossings

Crewmembers are offloading bales of seized marijuana from a drug-trafficking vessel located along the Texas border with a street value of $1 million. *Author's collection.*

The suspected marijuana is field tested at the dock with a narcotics identification kit (NIK) to quickly determine if the product is an illegal substance. *Author's collection.*

of goods, materials and alcohol were attempted frequently with little consequence prior to the 1919 Prohibition act. Today, the Coast Guard units at the Brazos Santiago Pass are enforcing and stopping the illegal trafficking of narcotics and illegal fishing by foreign vessels in U.S. waters.

The U.S. Coast Guard was moved from the Treasury Department to the Department of Transportation in the spring of 1967 and remained there until 2002 as a result of the 9-11 attacks. They were then reassigned to the Department of Homeland Security, where they remain to this day. The United States Coast Guard is the only military branch of service not assigned to the Department of Defense. Because it is the only branch that does not report to the Department of Defense, the Coast Guard can take on more missions that are not considered defense-related.

Being a border-based Coast Guard station, Station Port Isabel has been active in counternarcotic initiatives, as this area of responsibility is a known drug-trafficking corridor.

In 1982, the Department of Defense utilized Coast Guard law enforcement boarding parties on U.S. Navy ships to further the National Narcotics Border Interdiction System's (antinarcotic operations) mission. Coast Guard boarding officers were sent from Station Port Isabel as part of this defense effort for temporary duty on U.S. Navy ships for worldwide assignments.

Station Point Isabel (1923–1974)

With the U.S. Life-Saving Service and the U.S Revenue Cutter Service merging into the U.S. Coast Guard in 1915, the assessment of both ships and stations continued, and Coast Guard needs along the Texas border were addressed.

As a result of the hurricane destruction on the Brazos Santiago Station, it was decided that the station would not be rebuilt on Brazos Island. A new location on the south end of South Padre Island would be a more suitable location.

The Brazos Santiago Lighthouse was already located on South Padre Island, and the new Coast Guard station, Station Point Isabel, would also be on South Padre Island.

This new location was better in protecting the station from the direct impact of storms and hurricanes. The building was constructed from the blueprints of a standard "1903 Gulf Design." Most stations followed this style of being built on elevated pilings several feet above the ground all along the Gulf of Mexico. The building is a rectangular shape. The area between the pilings below the building served as a workspace and storage area for boats and equipment. The roof was a "hipped" style, with wide eaves providing for a 360-degree veranda. On top of the roof was a watchtower for watch standers to observe distressed vessels in need of assistance. It was

The station was constructed on pilings at the base of the dunes. The walkway on the left led to the boathouse and moorings. *USCG Station SPI collection.*

The communications room was staffed in four-hour periods. Note the coffee cup, a must for long hours of working the radios and phone. *Author's collection.*

built on pilings almost twelve feet above ground in an effort to protect it from high tidal storm surges. As of this writing, the building is still standing, making it nearly one hundred years old.

The station was modern by 1920s standards and came with a power plant for emergencies; the lookout tower was on the roof above the attic, and it had a walkway on all four sides. This aided the station keeper and crew in keeping a sharp watch on the weather and vessels in peril. The facility was complete with a dining (mess) hall, dormitory rooms, administrative offices and a radio/teletype room.

The station's site location was a large sandy "flats" area, easily influenced by the tide. The station was constructed well inland to be clear of any spring (higher than average) tidal flooding. This required the boat moorings to be approximately three-hundred yards east of the station, at the edge of navigable waters. The boat moorings were within one hundred feet of the Brazos Santiago Lighthouse. There was a long wooden pier between the new station and the boat moorings.

The station was completed in 1923. CWO Wallace L. Reed was the first officer in charge. In 1928, with the hope of a deep-water port coming to the area, Point Isabel was renamed Port Isabel, and the Coast Guard followed suit by changing the station's name to U.S. Coast Guard Station Port Isabel.

This building was an active Coast Guard station for fifty-one years.

Building the Jetties (1928)

The north and south jetties were completed in 1928 by the U.S. Army Corps of Engineers. The present location of the jetties was influenced by the 1860–70s railroad pier. The railroad pier had been used to remove cargo from ships making their way to the Brazos Santiago Pass. The huge granite-cut stones were put into place through a trestle rail system, allowing the trestle system to be extended as each jetty was extended.

Offshore from the Brazos Santiago Pass sits the Brazos Santiago Sea Buoy, with a light and a wave-activated whistle. This buoy is in place to alert mariners that they are nearing South Padre Island's jetties. At the tip of the north jetty sits a red buoy with a red blinking light and a wave-activated bell. Just off the south jetty sits a green buoy with a white blinking

The north and south jetties provide a safe passage in and out of the Brazos Santiago Pass, protecting mariners from harsh sea conditions. *USCG Station SPI collection.*

light and a wave-activated gong. This provides an audio and visual means to alert mariners of the South Padre Island jetties. The buoys were placed there by the U.S. Coast Guard as a means to ensure the safe transit in and out of this now-man-made and maintained passage.

CHIEF PABLO VALENT:
HISPANIC AMERICAN LEADER AND HERO (1935)

Chief Pablo Valent was the first Hispanic American person to lead a rescue station, Coast Guard Station Port Isabel in 1935. He was no stranger to the Brazos Santiago Pass, as he had served under Station Keeper Wallace L. Reed some fifteen years earlier and was part of the boat crew that had received the Silver Life-Saving Medal for rescuing eight sailors from the schooner *Cape Horn* on September 16, 1919.

On March 2, 2018, the new Coast Guard Corpus Christi Sector building was named Valent Hall in honor of him. Chief Valent was a native of Corpus Christi. A new 123-foot-long fast response Sentinel-class cutter is being built that will bear his name: Coast Guard cutter *Pablo Valent* (WPC-1148).

Chief Valent retired in 1940, having served for more than twenty-eight years with both the life-saving service and the U.S. Coast Guard. He remained in South Texas and was an active community member in the Brownsville area.

Chief Boatswain's Mate Pablo Valent, the first Hispanic person to serve as the officer-in-charge of Station Port Isabel, Texas. *USCG Station SPI collection.*

ORAL HISTORY INTERVIEW WITH LCDR
CHARLES R. WILSON USCG (RETIRED) (1948)

This oral history interview took place in 2021; Commander Wilson was ninety-two years old and spoke of World War II events that occurred seventy years ago as if they happened yesterday. Some of the content was edited to protect the privacy of his shipmates. It was my pleasure to interview him.

AUTHOR. Commander Wilson, thank you for your time today. Before accepting a commission, you had enlisted and were an engineer stationed in South Texas with the Coast Guard on South Padre Island. Can you tell us what that was like for you and what memories stand out in your experiences of having served there?

COMMANDER WILSON. I came to Port Isabel Lifeboat Station in the fall of 1948. I passed through Los Fresnos before I learned later that it was a town. A filling station and a general store at the crossroads, with about six houses (shacks) was all that made the town. After passing through Los Fresnos, a stretch of land for about eighteen miles with cactus, wiregrass and mesquite trees littered the scenery. I learned later that this area, south of Highway 100 to Brownsville, was known as "Jack Ass Flats," named for it's thickly populated wild jack asses that were turned loose or abandoned during the turn of the twentieth century. This highway to Port Isabel was straight as a highway could be except for two turns. One, a sharp 90-degree turn with a fertilizer plant on the turn that used scrap fish for its material and smelled to high heaven. Another long sweeping turn that put you back on to the direction of Port Isabel.

At Laguna Vista, San Jose Road (County Road 510) intersected with Highway 100. There were about three houses at this intersection at that time with the Coast Guard radio station. This station was constructed during World War II because communications to this region were very limited. This station's radio transmission was very powerful and capable of communicating with Coast Guard Station New Orleans. The officer in charge was a first-class radioman. It was a one-man family station, and the petty officer had his family living with him.

Port Isabel was primarily a fishing boat port—shrimp being a major product. Tourists came to spend a day of fishing on charter boats. Maw and Paw Sullivan had a large yacht, and Collier's Boat Service had several smaller boats used for this purpose. Collier also had a barge used to carry small vehicles to the island, as there was no causeway.

As best that I can recall, Port Isabel had had, among other things, a grocery store (Light House Grocery), a filling station, the Queen Isabella Hotel, a yacht club and hotel and several places for rent. My wife and I had one child at this time, and we rented a cottage at the hotel for a while and, later, a small duplex.

As stated, there was no causeway to the island, so all transportation to and from the island was via boat. The Coast Guard station had one twenty-five-

Left: LCDR Charles R. Wilson and Bertha "Birdie" Wilson. *Author's collection.*

Below: All that remains are the concrete pads on which Port Isabel Lifeboat Station sat; they can be seen in the brush, next to the intersection's local convenient store. *LCDR C.R. Wilson's collection.*

foot utility boat called the A-to-N boat for aids to navigation; one thirty-eight-foot picket boat with a 6-71 GM diesel engine, speed about twenty knots; one thirty-six-foot lifeboat, a double-ended wood hull with 2,500 pounds of a brass keel for righting itself in rough seas, this boat had a maximum speed of six knots, but it was a very good boat for towing and maintaining stability in rough seas; one surf boat with oars and no engine, used for launching from the beach and rescue services for stranded or grounded vessels.

When I arrived, only the A-to-N boat was running. This was not necessarily the fault of the personnel responsible to maintain the boats. The Coast Guard, at this time, was broke. Not much money. Personnel were not paid for two months in 1949. Congress did not fund the military

Above: An aerial view of the Coast Guard property on South Padre Island. The boathouse is in the foreground, and the station building is in the background. *CWO3 D. Cook's collection.*

Opposite: Horses played a critical role in patrolling long stretches of beach during times of war, peace and search-and-rescue efforts—Semper Paratus (Always Ready)! *USCG Station SPI collection.*

services to the level needed to maintain machinery and logistics. New parts for engines were next to nonexistent. I was an engineer responsible for, among other things, fixing what was broke. When necessary, I fixed things by making parts and making them work—modifying parts made for other machinery to fit what I had. Eventually, I got all boats running and ready for duty.

The CG station had telephone service to the Port Isabel's telephone landline. This line was installed during the World War II era along with a line about twenty miles up the island that was used by the beach patrol personnel during the war. This patrol used the line to report their position and any unusual activities. Interesting to note that the patrol personnel rode on horses.

Beach patrol of World War II

Another interesting note was the hotel on the beach, about two miles north of the north jetty, which was demolished during the 1919 tropical storm, it had been restored well enough to house one person whom I never met and who had nothing to do with anyone on the island. Talk about a hermit.

The Coast Guard station had a chief petty officer in charge. I got off to a bad start with him the day I reported aboard because I addressed him as "hey chief." He didn't like that. I later found out why; he was a warrant officer during World War II, and he got busted back to chief when the war ended. Because he was the officer in charge, he wanted to be addressed as "sir." It didn't happen.

He didn't spend much time on the station. I later read the log, which was a daily record of station events. He was always doing Coast Guard business with civilian businesses or companies. Actually, he was at his house in Port Isabel doing nothing. He got his just award when he authorized a civilian electrical firm in Brownsville to do extensive work on Coast Guard electronic equipment without authority. He got a real good letter of reprimand from the commandant of the Coast Guard through the chain of command, stating, among other things, that he would never make warrant officer (his wartime rank), and he was transferred to another unit. With him gone, I re-enlisted for six years.

The station was totally disorganized under the chief's leadership, and the matter was known in the district office. As a result, they sent LTJG James A. Alsup as commanding officer of the station. He had been a first-class petty officer before the war started and in charge of another lifeboat station on the Texas coast. During World War II, he was promoted to lieutenant, then demoted to lieutenant, junior grade. after the war ended. Mr. Alsup and I worked well together from day one. The crew of thirteen men had duty, six days on the island and two days off, with one night off in between liberties. Morale was as high as one could expect under the conditions and far superior than it was under the previous command.

AUTHOR. Commander Wilson, it sounds like leadership was important then, as it is today. Now that you had the boats running and a good leader at the station, what about search-and-rescues (SAR)? I bet that was exciting times.

COMMANDER WILSON. We did have our anxious times. I made first-class petty officer soon after Mr. Alsup arrived on board. Our search-and-rescue activity increased to as many as twenty-three missions per month. This was because of Mr. Alsup's dedication to duty, not because there was more need. Word got around that help was available if needed from the Coast Guard under the new command. We had an eighty-three-foot patrol boat that moored at the ship basin docks in Port Isabel that had its own crew. They got a call one foggy morning of a shrimp boat running aground just south of the ship channel jetties. The fog was thick that night, and they saw a jetty and thought they were in the channel. The eighty-three-footer attempted to get a line on the shrimp boat and, in the process, pounced on a submerged piling that has been left when the jetties were laid. The damage was two holes in the engine room, yet the cutter managed to the beach inside the jetties on the north side of the channel. This allowed the station crew better and easier access to assist the cutter's crew. We managed to cover the holes with canvas and get it to a dry dock for repairs.

About three nights later, we got a SAR call from a shrimp boat that was broke down about three miles south of the jetties, out in the gulf. Our thirty-six-foot lifeboat was deployed with a first-class petty officer, an engineer and a deckhand to assist. About halfway through the jetties, the lifeboat rammed a small shrimp boat with no running lights. The shrimp boat sank, and a first-class petty officer dived in the rapid current water and pulled the lone shrimper to safety.

Shortly after these two events, inspectors from the district office were in Port Isabel for a board of investigation; Mr. Alsup and the first-class petty officer involved in the collision were in attendance. I was left in charge of the station during the commanding officer's absence. One of my shipmates, a first-class petty officer that I worked with daily, had had overnight liberty the previous day and returned to the station about 0800 this day. He was my peer, and we usually planned the day's work together. This a.m. was very different and unusual. He failed to secure the boat to the dock when he arrived, which was not like him at all. He was usually very thorough in this respect. He went to the lookout tower and asked the man on the watch to borrow his sidearm. Being refused, he asked the man on watch to shoot him. This was not happening; he proceeded to the station from the boathouse, passing me without a word. This being most unusual, I went to the lookout tower and checked with the man on watch, and I was updated on the events. I saw the boat adrift in the boat basin. Putting these events together, I called the station mess deck, where I knew the crew would be, and ordered a search for the troubled crewman. He was later found—dead, as he had hanged himself in the station building's attic.

AUTHOR. Commander Wilson, that had to be a devastating time for you and the crew, as he was a shipmate, a friend.

COMMANDER WILSON. Yes, and all disasters must be investigated. It was discovered that he was having marital issues and could no longer cope with the magnitude of it all.

Port Isabel was, at that time, a very small town, and everyone seemed to know everyone else's business. I called the phone switchboard operator in Port Isabel and told her what had happened and to find Mr. Alsup and pass the information. In no time, all of Port Isabel knew what had happened, and Mr. Alsup was on his way to the station.

You would think that all of this would be enough, but no, there is more, as the lookout watch standers would sleep in the attic of the boathouse where the lookout tower was located. There was a head, a toilet in the attic and plenty of room for a temporary barracks. It was summertime, and the nights were almost as hot as the days, and there was no air conditioning. One of the watch standers, a young man known by the crew to be jumpy or easy to scare, was just relieved of his watch at 0400. The first thing one does after a watch is go to the head and then sack out. He did this; only, when he turned on the light in the head, he saw a dummy-figure hanging from the rafters. Seeing this, he screamed and ran the three hundred yards to the station. After the long run, he had calmed some, but it still did some internal injury. The crew members that were responsible for this demeanor forever regretted their actions.

AUTHOR. Commander Wilson, thank you for sharing such a personal story about your shipmate. It sounds like roughhousing and practical jokes were a way for the crew to cope with the devastation. What rescues stand out for you while being stationed at the Port Isabel Station?

COMMANDER WILSON. One night during my tour on the island, Mr. Alsup, me and one of the other crew members were playing cards when the lookout watchman called and reported that he thought he saw flames coming from a shrimp boat tied to the old railroad piling at the south jetty. Mr. Alsop, being the dedicated man, wanted to take nothing for granted. We loaded portable fire extinguishers on the picket boat and headed for the shrimp boat. We were underway in about three minutes after receiving the call. No flames were seen until we got about fifty yards from the boat. We boarded the shrimp boat, set off the fire extinguishers, dropped them in the burning compartment, and went back to the station for more firefighting equipment. I had the water pump running when we got back to the shrimp boat. All of this was done in about thirty minutes. The extinguishers had almost put the fire out. If not for the extinguishers, we may have lost the boat. As it was, the fire was extinguished, and the boat was repaired and back in service.

AUTHOR. Commander Wilson, it sounds like you all—the crew—were a close-knit group?

COMMANDER WILSON. Yes, when I got orders to report to Santa Rosa Lifeboat Station in Florida, the same unit that the former chief in charge was stationed. He wasn't the officer in charge, but he was there, and I definitely didn't want to see or serve with him. To my way of thinking, the service doesn't need his kind. Mr. Alsup knew my feelings toward this man, and he went out on a limb to get my orders canceled. This didn't do his career any good, and he knew it. I stayed at Port Isabel for another year when I received orders for isolated duty in Alaska. Mr. Alsup was promoted to lieutenant and assigned as executive officer on the CGC *Iris*. He was not only my commanding officer, but he, his wife and his family became good friends of me, my wife and my family.

During the time I was stationed at Port Isabel Lifeboat Station, we had a crew complement of thirteen men, one officer. Our mission was approximately 80 percent search-and-rescue, 15 percent aids to navigation and 5 percent law enforcement. While I was in Alaska, a new lifeboat station commanding officer was assigned, and about March of 1951, the boathouse burned down.

The city of Port Isabel can be seen in the foreground, with the burning of Coast Guard facilities in the background. The Point Isabel Lighthouse is to the left. *BMCM A. Pechacek's collection.*

Nothing was saved because of the failure of the fire extinguishing system. During this year, 1951, the first causeway was built from the mainland of Port Isabel to South Padre Island. Because of that causeway and, now, the new causeway, both named Queen Isabella, the island has populated and grown into a popular tourist attraction.

AUTHOR. Commander Wilson, I appreciate you using this interview to pay respect to your peer, your friend and share your recollections.

You mentioned getting stationed after this in Alaska, and I know you went on to serve a remarkable career in the Coast Guard for more than twenty-seven years. How did you come to join the U.S. Coast Guard? Please share with us your decision, recruit training and those early experiences.

COMMANDER WILSON. On April 12, 1946, I enlisted in the United States Coast Guard. I was a green seventeen-year-old kid, a school dropout that had no directions, no forethought as to my future living in McKinney, Texas. I was just looking forward to a different way of life. I played hooky from school one day and hitched a ride to Dallas. I went to some county building where all the service recruiting offices were located. There were several other

Coast Guard recruit Charlie Wilson during bootcamp training. *LCDR C.R. Wilson's collection.*

guys there waiting for the doors to open. All of them wanted to go into the Navy. The Navy wouldn't take them because McKinney's recruiting office was open on Thursdays; this was a Monday. Two guys went with me to the Coast Guard office. We filled out papers; the recruiter sent us to a clinic close by for a physical. I passed; the other two didn't. I went back to the recruiter and took the entrance test. I passed the Coast Guard aptitude test, and they sent me home for my parents' signature. Dad and Mom reluctantly signed. I hiked it back to the Dallas recruiting office the next day with my papers and a small suitcase.

I was sworn in for three years, given meal tickets and a travel voucher via a train to Baltimore, Maryland. My first time to ride a train in a Pullman car. The bootcamp was at Curtis Bay, a short distance from Baltimore. When the train entered the train station, I experienced the strangest smell in the atmosphere that I had ever had—the burning of coal. I'll never forget that smell.

Someone picked me up at the train station and took me to Curtis Bay. I was taken to a barracks where I gave my papers to a guy in uniform and was told to find a bunk—but don't sit on it. Stand or sit on the floor. This barracks was a two-story frame building that housed forty-two bunks down and forty-two bunks up with a head on each floor and a company commander quarters, usually a petty officer. There were six or eight guys there in civilian clothes, just sitting. I soon found out that this was the routine until a company was formed. A company consisted of eighty-four men. It took about a week for this to happen. We marched to the small stores, where we were issued our uniforms and all other paraphernalia that we were to maintain. The first thing we did was go back to the barracks, make a stencil with our name and serial number and stencil every piece of clothing and/or equipment that was issued, including the sewing kit. With these in hand, we were directed to send everything else that we brought back home. We started our training. At first, it was marching and running. I picked up the marching pretty quick because of the ROTC training we had in high school. I was blocks ahead of the company and the instructors on the running because I had just finished football spring training before I joined up. The instructors looked at me as if I was something special. I didn't want to stand out, so I held back after that first run. I never saw so many young guys so out of shape. We used Saturdays to wash our clothes. We had no washer. Just a rub-board, a bucket, soap and a brush. Hung clothes on close line to dry. If they were not stenciled with our name on them, we lost them.

After the first week of running and marching, we started rowing the lifeboat. Ten guys with a helmsman rowing a twenty-five-foot rowboat. Old fashion but effective.

After about three weeks, we were ordered to fall out on the grass side of the barracks. We usually fall out on the street side. There was a lieutenant, a chief warrant officer and a chief petty officer there to inspect the company and two other companies. These three walked down each line of boots, and he would point to one and tell him to fall out to the street side of the barracks. We had no idea what was going on. They passed me and turned around and came back and told me to fall out and line up with the others. They picked fifty boots for their project. Finally, the lieutenant told us that Curtis Bay Training Camp was being closed, and the Coast Guard was opening a new boot camp in Mayport, Florida, at a naval air and aircraft station. We were to be the crew to open this station for recruit training. We gathered up our gear, boarded a train and headed for Florida.

When we got settled in the barracks, the chief warrant officer and the chief petty officer came through the ranks, looking for people to certain jobs. Guys that had any training in about any field was open and needed. Some of the guys I got close to in this short time went to station police jobs like gate guards and fence patrol. I didn't particularly care for this type of job. Those that didn't get picked for a job went to the galley as mess cooks, where they cleaned up after the cooks. I had mentioned to someone that I had driven a school bus to take football players home after practice when in high school. After about three days in the galley, I heard someone call my name from afar. I showed up to find that Mr. Limon, the lieutenant, wanted the guy that had school bus experience. That's me. They needed someone to take the liberty party to Jacksonville Beach and make bus runs into the Jacksonville Train Station to pick up Coasties being transferred to Mayport. At first, the bus was a top-heavy vehicle, like a box-type milk truck that had beaches running parallel on each side with handles for one to hold on to if there were no seats. Later, I graduated to a thirty-seven-passenger bus similar to a school bus. My duties were to run scheduled trips to the USO in Jacksonville Beach about four times a day. I had twenty-four hours on duty and twenty-four hours off.

AUTHOR. Commander Wilson, I appreciate you taking the time to share with us and for permission to use your story as part of *The Coast Guard on the Texas Border* collection. Thank you.

COMMANDER WILSON. You are most welcome; it has been my privilege.

Dredging of the Intracoastal Waterway (1949)

The Coast Guard has a responsibility for protecting and marking the federal navigable waterways. It maintains these waterways through its aids to navigation fleet and units strategically placed across the United States and its territories. It is commonly referred to as the "black fleet," as all of the vessel hulls are painted black. This is a term of endearment, as many Coast

One dredge digging north, the other digging south. There are a few remaining yards to connect South Texas to the Intracoastal Waterway, all the way to New Jersey. *USCG Station SPI collection.*

Guard members take pride in having served a career in the black fleet. This dedicated group of hardworking men and women are responsible for the natural waterways, such as the Mississippi River, and also man-made canals, such as the Intracoastal Waterway.

In 1909, Congress passed the Rivers and Harbors Act for a formal intracoastal waterway system from Massachusetts to Cameron County, Texas. This act provided safe navigation of goods and people, protecting them from open-sea passages where possible. The Intracoastal Waterway (ICW) is comprised of natural waterways and dredged canals, spanning approximately three thousand nautical miles.

The southernmost end of the Intracoastal Waterway terminates in Cameron County, Texas, at the Brownsville Ship Channel. The southernmost dredging to complete the planned ICW system began in December 1945 and continued through the planned 150-mile dredging through the Laguna Madre Bay. The laguna is a protected body of water between the mainland of Texas to its west and the barrier island South Padre Island to its east. The average depth of the laguna is considered to be 3 feet at mean tide. The ICW was dredged for a depth of 12 feet and a width of 125 feet for its 150-mile length, including the "mud flats" area that separated the Lower and Upper Laguna Madre. In June 1949, the channel was completed and has been in operation ever since.

Today, the Coast Guard's aids to navigation team (ATON) on South Padre Island maintains the southernmost end of the ICW, servicing more than 373 buoys and markers.

Brownsville Ship Channel Opens (1936)

The Roaring Twenties brought Cameron County new roads, and old roads became paved roads, with all roads leading to a newly built international bridge for automotive passage to and from Mexico. The railways were continuing to grow, and Brownsville saw a boom due to a renewed interest in real estate investments.

In an effort to bring more port trade to Cameron County and specifically to Brownville, it was decided by way of a $2 million bond to bring the maritime industry to the area in the way of a Brownsville Ship Channel and Port. A seventeen-mile channel was dredged from the Brazos Santiago Pass to Brownsville. The new channel was thirty-six feet deep and two hundred feet wide, with an even larger turning basin at the channel's end. The Brownsville Ship Channel was completed on May 15, 1936.

The U.S. Coast Guard safety inspectors were responsible for the marine inspection of vessels entering the new ship channel. The Coast Guard aids to navigation team was responsible for adding and maintaining the entrance buoys, navigational markers and channel range towers. Today, there are approximately forty aids to navigation lights, plus additional buoys and markers within the seventeen-mile-long Brownsville Ship Channel.

In the Brownsville Ship Channel, the Coast Guard maintained a moorings facility for Coast Guard cutters homeported in the area. The moorings were created in 1964 on nearly seven acres of waterfront property on Oil Dock Road. Initially, this was home to three of the 125-foot-long cutters: the *McLane*, the *Kimball* and the *Boutwell*. It was also home to the Coast Guard

Top: Coast Guard dock and moorings in the Brownsville Ship Channel. *MkC B. Eason's collection.*

Bottom: The CGC *Durable* (WMEC-628) moored in the Port of Brownsville. *CWO3 D. Cook's collection.*

marine safety detachment. In 1967, it became the homeport for the cutter *Durable*. In the late 1970s, a tennis court was installed on the property. In the late 1980s, the facilities were no longer needed, as the *Durable* was reassigned, and the installation eventually closed.

Marine Safety Detachment (MSD) Brownsville (1938)

As technological advances were made in traveling the waterways of the United States, the risk for mishap also increased, and a more formal inspection process was needed. Still, for decades, largely no action was taken. With legislation passed in 1838 and then again in 1852, the revenue cutter service was charged with inspecting the safety of vessels and later became the responsibility of the U.S. Coast Guard.

The safety of vessels coming into U.S. ports is a critical mission. As a result of many disasters and lives lost on unregulated steamboats, the Steamboat Act of 1852 was finally enacted but provided little in the way of making the waterways safe from steamboat mechanical explosions and mishaps. In 1871, Congress established the Steamboat Inspection Service.

This led the way for more formal maritime safety regulations, and in 1910, the Motorboat Act was put into place, requiring safety inspections on both commercial and private boats. In 1932, it was combined with the Bureau of Navigation, and in 1936, the Bureau of Navigation and Steamboat Inspection became the Bureau of Marine Inspection and Navigation. It was not until after World War II that Presidential Executive Order 9083 permanently made marine inspections a responsibility of the United States Coast Guard and, specifically, a requirement for Coast Guard marine safety offices and depots. As a result, Marine Safety Detachment Brownsville was established after the Port of Brownsville opened. It is responsible for inspecting ships entering and leaving the Brownsville Ship Channel and the Brazos Santiago Pass.

Auxiliary Flotilla 7-2 (1939)

Amid the New Deal, Congressional H.R. 5966 (the Coast Guard Reserve Act) was drafted and passed, and on June 23, 1939, President Franklin Roosevelt signed into law the creation of the U.S. Coast Guard Reserve.

The Coast Guard Reserve was founded as a volunteer, nonmilitary (civilian) group with the intended purpose of promoting safe boating practices to the increased recreational boating in the United States. It was an all-volunteer civilian initiative.

As the military's needs grew in the 1940s, the Coast Guard Reserve required participants to be subject to the 1775 Articles of War and Military

Right: Climbing a rope ladder along the hull of a foreign-flagged ship in order to complete a marine safety inspection of the vessel and cargo. *PSC A. Martinez's collection.*

Below: A team of Coast Guard auxiliary volunteers preparing to get underway and patrol the Brazos Santiago Pass. *Author's collection.*

Law. It was then that the all-volunteer civilian initiative of 1939 was renamed the U.S. Coast Guard Auxiliary.

The auxiliary is structured to maintain a presence within the United States and its territories through flotilla, division, district regions, and national representation. Since 1939, the auxiliary has played a vital role in promoting recreational boating safety. In 1997, it was authorized to volunteer for and participate in supporting all Coast Guard missions except direct military and law enforcement operations.

Coast Guard Auxiliary Flotilla 7-2 operates along the Texas border. This flotilla has the distinct prestige of being the oldest continuous flotilla within the division. Beginning in the 1940s, Flotilla 7-2 has supported recreational boating safety in the Laguna Madre area, the Brazos Santiago Pass and the Gulf of Mexico.

U.S. COAST GUARD RESERVES (1939)

The U.S. Coast Guard Reserves was born from an all-volunteer service of privately owned yachts and recreational boats, the U.S. Coast Guard Auxiliary.

The summer and fall of 1939 was a hectic time in our nation and, specifically, for the U.S. Coast Guard. One week after the Coast Guard Auxiliary was created, President Franklin Roosevelt, on July 1, 1939, absorbed the U.S. Lighthouse Service into the U.S. Coast Guard, stretching the leadership demands and resources.

On October 17, 1940, with the demands of the volunteer auxiliary increasing to protect our seaports, Congress introduced bills to reorganize the Coast Guard Reserve to function in the same military roles as the Navy Reserve and other reserve military branches. This required the original 1939 Coast Guard Reserve Act to be repealed. This allowed for the naming convention and responsibilities of the Coast Guard Auxiliary and the Coast Guard Reserve to be clearly defined. In response to World War II, on November 1, 1941, the Coast Guard was transferred from the Department of Treasury to the Department of the Navy. The auxiliary continued on as a volunteer organization, and the reserves became a military entity in the Coast Guard's ranks within the Department of the Navy.

The Coast Guard returned to the Treasury Department in December 1945.

Coast Guard Reserve Unit Port Isabel, Operating Facility (OPFAC) No. 08-82526, was established in the 1960s.

Left: Coast Guard Reserve Unit Port Isabel prepares a color guard detail to present the national colors at community presentations and military ceremonies. *YN3 D. Eason's collection.*

Below: The younger RK reservists completed boot camp between their junior and senior years of high school and are now in training with senior reservists. *BM3 L. (Alvarez) Valle's collection.*

The Active-Class Patrol Boats (1963–1969)

The Coast Guard cutter *McLane* was one of thirty-three active-class patrol boats built and commissioned beginning in 1927 to enforce Prohibition and smuggling. They were 125 feet in length and given the nickname "a buck and a quarter" class. The cutter *McLane* was decommissioned on December 31, 1968, and was one of the last of the three longest serving "buck and a quarter" boats. The other two were the cutters *Morris* and *Cuyahoga*. After decommissioning, the cutters *Morris* and *McLane* were given a new purpose in preserving history, with the cutter *McLane* being donated to the Great Lakes Naval Memorial and Museum and the cuter *Morris* donated to the Liberty Maritime Museum. Tragically, the cutter *Cuyahoga* was involved in an accident with another ship and sank on October 20, 1978.

The active-class 125-foot-long patrol boats were built in response to the ever-increasing need to support Prohibition in the early part of the twentieth century. Congress passed the National Prohibition Act in October 1919 to

The CGC *Kimball* (WSC-143) patrolling the Texas border. *USCG Station SPI collection.*

provide support and resources to enforce the Eighteenth Amendment, which called for the prohibition of alcohol. In 1933, the Eighteenth Amendment was repealed, and prohibition efforts were no longer required of the U.S. Coast Guard.

The cutter *Boutwell* (WSC-130) was commissioned on February 21, 1927, and assigned to prohibition duty, and its last homeport was Brownsville, Texas, where it conducted law enforcement patrols along the United States-Mexico border. The *Boutwell* was decommissioned on May 7, 1963. The cutter *McLane* (WSC-146) was commissioned on April 6, 1927, and was assigned to prohibition duty on the West Coast until 1933. It then continued serving on the West Coast and in Alaska on search-and-rescue and law enforcement missions, and from 1941 to 1946, it operated under the Navy to support World War II efforts. After the war, it continued service in both Alaska and Washington, and in 1966, it was assigned to Brownsville, Texas, where it spent its last assignment patrolling the Gulf of Mexico along the U.S. border. It was decommissioned in 1969. The cutter *Kimball* (WSC-143) was commissioned on May 7, 1927, and also served with its sister ships, the *McLane* and *Boutwell*, with prohibition duties along the Texas border. The *Kimball* was decommissioned on December 31, 1968.

AIDS TO NAVIGATION TEAM, PORT MANSFIELD, TEXAS (1963)

Red Fish Landing was a fish camp located on the northern Laguna Madre, a few miles south of Saltillo Flats, an area that was known for its fishing. In 1954, the U.S. Army Corps of Engineers dredged and improved the area. It was at this time that it was named Port Mansfield. The dredging continued, and in 1962, the final Port Mansfield Channel was completed, cutting across the barrier island—Padre Island. This man-made cut now separates North Padre Island from South Padre Island. It is commonly referred to as the East Cut.

Creating a Coast Guard aids to navigation team (ATON) at Port Mansfield served both the maintenance needs of the navigation aids for the East Cut and the Gulf Coast Intracoastal Waterway, and it also created a Coast Guard rescue presence on the northern boundary of Station Port Isabel's area of operation (AOR).

In 1963, the U.S. Coast Guard ATON Port Mansfield Facility was established. It consisted of a waterfront property with boat moorings and

The 1963 commissioning ceremony for the aids to navigation facility Port Mansfield. A large community turned out, and a local band played the national anthem. *USCG Station SPI collection.*

a modest aids to navigation building. Immediately adjacent to the station was a house for the crewmembers, and across the street from the station was Coast Guard housing in the way of a two-story duplex. The Coast Guard property located on both sides of Laguna Drive in Port Mansfield was the only property not owned by the Navigation District. The property on the west side of Laguna Drive at the Port Mansfield Harbor was the unit location, including its garages and moorings. There was also a building that was a bachelors' quarters and barracks for crewmembers. The buildings were built on a one-level concrete slab, which was uncharacteristic of the other Coast Guard piling structures that had been built along the Gulf Coast from the earliest days of the life-saving service.

Across the street on the east side of Laguna Drive was the two-story duplex. One of the homes was for the officer in charge, and the other for either the executive petty officer or the engineering petty officer. It was family housing, and those who had families and seniority dictated occupancy of those family quarters.

The unit had a fifty-five-foot-long aids to navigation boat (ANB), equipped with a work deck and crane for servicing the Intracoastal Waterway buoys. The ATON unit was responsible for all of the aids to navigation buoys, ranges, lights and markers on the Intracoastal Waterway

The ANB 55111 ATON boat passes through the ICW land cut, just north of Port Mansfield, Texas. *USCG Station SPI collection.*

between Brownsville, Texas, and the land cut at the Saltillo Flats. They would also service the offshore buoys at both Port Mansfield and the South Padre Island jetties.

In 1997, under BMC Rick Tupa's, the officer in charge, leadership, the unit was relocated to South Padre Island and renamed U.S. Coast Guard Aids to Navigation Team South Padre Island. Chief Tupa was the last officer in charge of ATON Port Mansfield. The old Port Mansfield buildings are now home to the Willacy County Navigation District.

LORAN A STATION PORT ISABEL (1967)

During World War II, there was a need for ship navigation to advance beyond visual navigation, dead reckoning and celestial navigation methods. While celestial navigation was accurate, it depended on a clear night, a clear line of sight for star gazing. This caused many hindrances to the war effort regarding missions and rendezvous locations of desperately needed supplies and troops. A long-range navigation (LORAN) electronic system was created out of that need and changed the method and accuracy of navigating forever. This required the design and construction of more than 150 transmitting stations around the world.

LORAN got its inspiration from following a similar electronic navigation example developed in the United Kingdom called Gee. Gee was a way of tracking your location through only electronic monitoring. The United States, under a top-secret mission, developed a better, more cost-effective system, the LORAN navigation system.

Prior to 1943, ships navigating off the coasts of the United States would do so by means of dead reckoning, a system of knowing one's current heading (direction), how fast they were going and recording the time. With this information, one could dead reckon from point A to point B. Dead reckoning, while functional, was not often reliable, as factors such as wind, seas and ocean current would drive the ship off course.

In the beginning of the 1940s, conversations were started around the idea of using an electronic broadcast signal to determine a more accurate location. As a result, the long-range navigation (LORAN) system was developed. LORAN is based on a chain or group of towers, as various locations will transmit signals that ships carrying LORAN recoverees could then plot an accurate position of their location.

In 1943, the first LORAN stations were placed along the northeastern shores of the United States and southeastern coasts of Canada. This chain of LORAN stations' success led to more and more stations being constructed across the United States and other countries to increase maritime and aviation navigation accuracy. While there was an Air Force–operated low-frequency LORAN chain in the Gulf of Mexico as a result of World War II, it was not until 1955 that the Coast Guard assumed responsibility for the LORAN chain and signals. The LORAN chain did not cover the entire gulf area at that time. As a response to promoting the commercial fishermen's safety, especially those on shrimp boats, a LORAN A station was installed on South Padre Island, Coast Guard LORAN Station Port Isabel.

As technology advances were made, the technology of LORAN also improved. They were initially called LORAN or LORAN A, then LORAN B (very briefly) and, finally, LORAN C. LORAN C navigation became available to anyone with a receiver, from pleasure boaters and private aviators to commercial airlines and commercial ships.

An aerial view of the Coast Guard Loran A Station located on South Padre Island, circa the 1970s. *USCG Station SPI collection.*

The United States Coast Guard was responsible for manning and maintaining the LORAN stations. Loran Station Port Isabel was established in 1967 and was in service until 1979, when it was replaced by LORAN C, being broadcast from the Coast Guard Station LORAN Raymondville.

THE POINT-CLASS PATROL BOATS (1967–1998)

The Coast Guard built seventy-nine Point-class cutters from 1960 to 1970. Each Cutter was eighty-two feet long with a steel hull and aluminum superstructure, with a nearly six-foot draft. They were designed for near-coastal use in support of search-and-rescue and law enforcement missions. In 1965 and 1966, twenty-six of the Point-class cutters were assigned to Vietnam. In 1969 and 1970, all of those cutters were transferred from the Coast Guard to the South Vietnamese navy. The remaining fifty-three Point-class cutters were assigned to home ports where Coast Guard stations already existed to support the local and near-coastal missions.

Top: CGC *Point Baker* (WPB-82342). *USCG Station SPI collection.*

Bottom: Conducting .50-caliber machine gun exercises along the Texas border. *Author's collection.*

The CGC *Point Baker* (WPB-82342) was commissioned on October 30, 1963, at the Coast Guard shipyard in Curtis Bay, Maryland. The commissioning crew and plank owners sailed it from Maryland down the East Coast to Florida and across the Gulf of Mexico to Texas, to its home on South Padre Island. In 1965, the CGC *Point Baker* was reassigned from the border area to its new homeport at Station Port Aransas, just north of Corpus Christi, Texas.

CGC *Point Nowell* (WPB-82363) on patrol between the Brazos Santiago Pass and the Texas border. *BMCM J. Caldwell's collection.*

The CGC *Point Nowell* (WPB-82363) was commissioned on June 13, 1967, in Tacoma, Washington. The commissioning crew and plank owners were listed:

BMCS Ambrose A. PECHACEK, officer in charge
ENCP M.R. MANGUM, engineering petty officer
BM1 W.R. THOMPSON, executive petty officer
CS2 R.K. ERICKSON, commissary
EN3 R.D. MCLASSON, engineering
SA H.A. BUDHANAN, deck force
SA J.W. WILSON, deck force
FA L.P. DELIKAT, engineering

The *Point Nowell* gets its name from a geographical point of land in Alaska, but the cutter served in one homeport for its entire thirty-year career: Station Port Isabel, located on South Padre Island, Texas.

The original eight, the plank owner crew of the CCC *Point Nowell*. *BMCM A. Pechacek's collection.*

Under BMCS Pechacek's leadership, the commissioning crew received the *Point Nowell* in Tacoma, Washington, and sailed it down the west coast of Washington, Oregon, California, the Baja California Peninsula, Mexico, Guatemala, El Salvador, Nicaragua, Costa Rica and Panama. At La Boca, Panama, it entered into the Panama Canal, making its way east. After exiting the Panama Canal, then on the eastern side of Panama, the crew continued sailing it up the east coast of Panama, Costa Rica, Nicaragua, Honduras, Mexico and Texas, to its home on South Padre Island.

The CGC *Point Nowell's* unofficial motto was, "Law and order on the border!" Among its many accomplishments was that of fisheries enforcement along the United States border with Mexico. In 1991, under the leadership

Above: These seized nets catch any aquatic wildlife in their path. Removing the nets was a priority for the "mighty *Point Nowell*" crew. *BMCM J. Caldwell's collection.*

Left: The 1991 National Marine Fisheries Service, Cooperative Unit of the Year Award for outstanding achievement in fisheries enforcement, presented to the *Point Nowell*. *BMCM J. Caldwell's collection.*

of BMCM James R. Caldwell, officer in charge, the "Mighty *Point Nowell*" received the National Marine Fisheries award for conducting more fisheries boardings, Lacy Act missions, net seizures and law enforcement procedures than any other Coast Guard cutter or station in the Eighth Coast Guard District. It's an accomplishment that ships almost three times its size could not compare to.

The CGC *Point Nowell* received the following Coast Guard Meritorious Unit Commendation (CGMUC) on February 19, 1992:

> *For meritorious service from April 1, 1992 to December 1, 1991, during which CGC* Point Nowell *met all programmed goals, completed 271 boardings, identified 1,036 safety violations, seized 54 nets that were not in compliance with Turtle Excluder Device (TED) regulations, arrested 14 vessel masters for prosecution, made 21 cases for Lacey Act violations and actively enforced the Texas shrimp closure during the summers of 1990 and 1991. The CGC* Point Nowell *prosecuted 16 search-and-rescue cases, assisted eight persons in distress, and saved or assisted property valued in excess of $286K. In December 1990, CGC* Point Nowell *responded to the disabled fishing vessel CAPT GIANG II, 90 miles offshore in 12-foot seas and 35-knot winds. Despite an inoperative surface search radar and lack of communications with the disabled vessel, the crew of CGC* Point Nowell *located the vessel, innovatively devised a safe towing arrangement and brought the stricken vessel safely to port. Throughout two intensive periods of the Texas shrimp closure, CGC* Point Nowell *aggressively patrolled the U.S./Mexico border in conjunction with an AEROSTAT and WMEC to board and inspect all shrimpers for compliance. CGC* Point Nowell *also enforced Lacey Act regulations on U.S. fishing vessels identified by the AEROSTAT in Mexico's waters. CGC* Point Nowell *was a leader throughout the Gulf of Mexico this period in enforcing TED and fishing regulations while always looking for drugs and safety violations. This made CGC* Point Nowell *an extremely effective unit, earning respect from all commercial seamen in South Texas. The devotion to duty and excellent performance of CGC* Point Nowell *personnel are in keeping with the highest traditions of the United States Coast Guard.*
>
> *The Operational Distinguishing Device is authorized.*

On October 15, 1999, the *Point Nowell* was decommissioned and transferred to Jamaica, where it was renamed the *Savanna Point*.

Reliance-Class Cutters (1969–1986)

The Reliance-class cutters were 210-foot-long medium endurance ships. The Reliance-class were placed into service from 1964 to 1969 in an effort to replace the aging cutters that had been built for the Prohibition efforts. There were sixteen Reliance cutters put into service. They were air-conditioned, with crew accommodations for more extended deployments. The cutters were designed for six- to eight-week patrols, complete with a flight deck for launching and receiving helicopters at sea in an effort to further the search-and-rescue and law enforcement missions of the U.S. Coast Guard.

The Reliance-class cutters all have names that inspire courage, drive and are characteristic of dedication, hence the names: *Reliance, Diligence, Vigilant, Active, Confidence, Resolute, Valiant, Courageous, Steadfast, Dauntless, Venturous, Dependable, Vigorous, Durable, Decisive* and *Alert*.

The CGC *Durable* (WMEC-628) was commissioned at the Coast Guard shipyard in Baltimore, Maryland, on April 29, 1967. It was immediately placed into service in Galveston, Texas, and a year later, in 1968, its new homeport was Brownsville, Texas, taking over for the CCG *McLane*, one of

The crew of the CGC *Durable* passing time on the bow between operations and boardings along the Texas border. *CWO3 D. Cook's collection.*

The CGC *Durable* (WMEC-628) on her moorings in South Texas. *CWO3 D. Cook's collection.*

the last cutters that had been built in the Prohibition era. The CGC *Durable* remained in Brownsville, Texas, for the next seventeen years.

In 1986, it was decommissioned and sent back to the East Coast to be completely overhauled. It was one of several ships accepted into the shipyard's Major Maintenance Availability Program. Once the overhaul was complete, the CGC *Durable* was placed back into service in Florida in 1989.

STATION PORT ISABEL ADMINISTRATION BUILDING AND BARRACKS (1974)

The 1923 Coast Guard building that Station Port Isabel crews were operating in had become overcrowded, very outdated and dilapidated over its last fifty-plus years of use. Plans were made for a new administration building that was to be located closer to the waterfront facility. Over the years, the Coast Guard property's low tide areas on South Padre Island had been filled in with dredged material from the Brazos Santiago Pass, Brownsville Ship Channel and the local Sea Ranch Marina. This provided an ideal location for the new building. In 1974, the new building was completed and housed the latest technology for a communications center, galley, berthing and administration offices. This new building was constructed on stilts to hurricane standards and has been in service for more than forty-seven years. It was updated again in 2020.

Top: The 1974 administration building and barracks. *USCG Station SPI collection.*

Bottom: The commissioning crew mustered on the recreation deck of the 1974 facility. *USCG Station SPI collection.*

LORAN C STATION RAYMONDVILLE (1978)

Coast Guard LORAN Station Raymondville was established in September 1978. The LORAN antenna stood seven hundred feet above the surrounding farm and cattle land of Raymondville in Willacy County. LORAN Station Raymondville was part of the Southeast U.S. LORAN Chain (No. 7980) and was declared operational one month later in October 1978.

The facilities at LORAN Station Raymond were an operations building and office and a housing building. The operations building was a flat-roofed building that was constructed on a concrete slab. Because of the electronics equipment needed, the building had three firewalls in the event of an emergency. The crewmembers lived in a one-story ranch-style home at the entrance to the property, and there was a small antenna for communicating with the operations building and with local HAM (amateur radio) operators.

LORAN provided pulsed, low-frequency, hyperbolic, long-range navigation aid to ships and aircraft. The signals worked through a system of towers that transmitted radio signals, which could be received and plotted from three or more towers. By doing so, a ship or aircraft could determine its position over hundreds of miles to within one hundred feet of accuracy.

In 1979, a ghost was reported coming out of LORAN Station Raymondville, but it was not your typical ghoul or goblin ghost. Instead, it was a false signal, a ghost signal that, in many cases, when observed on ship receivers, could indicate a position of errors upward of two to three hundred kilometers. Brownsville and Port Isabel are large shrimp boat ports. The local fishermen relied heavily on LORAN C navigation in order to remain in U.S. waters along the border of Mexico and Texas.

It was determined that the Raymondville ghost signal's likely source was the result of the primary LORAN signal from Raymondville reflecting off of the Sierra Madre Mountains in Mexico and then back toward the Port Isabel/Brownsville area. The Coast Guard reported the ghosting problem, and ship receivers in the area were modified, but the ghost of Raymondville continued haunting the unknowing navigators of the southern end of the Gulf of Mexico along the Texas border.

Main entrance sign to LORAN Station Raymondville. *A. Dart's collection.*

Above: The LORAN mechanical and signal generating building. On the left is the base of the tower. *A. Dart's collection.*

Left: The tower, reaching seven hundred feet into the sky, is heavily secured with multiple guide wires. It could be seen for miles across the South Texas plains. *A. Dart's collection.*

LORAN Station Raymondville was essential to Coast Guard vessels and aircraft performing search-and-rescue missions and Lacy Act enforcement along the Texas border. The Lacy Act does not allow for the taking or transporting of any fish or wildlife from another country into the United States. The LORAN signal being broadcast from Station Raymondville allowed for a more accurate determination of vessels that may be in violation of the Lacy Act. It also served as a valuable navigation tool for fishermen to better know their location so they could abide by the law and maintain legal fishing positions along the South Texas border.

LORAN progressed through its life cycle as LORAN A, LORAN B (mostly a testing phase) and LORAN C, with C being the longest phase for a total signal broadcast of sixty-seven years, eight months and twenty-four days. On February 8, 2010, the Coast Guard ended transmissions of all U.S. LORAN C signals. As global positioning satellite (GPS) navigation technology became available, it surpassed the accuracy of and need for LORAN stations.

TEXAS SOUTHMOST COLLEGE TAKES OVER 1923 STATION (1987)

In 1987, the board of trustees at Texas Southmost College designated the Historical 1923 Coast Guard Station as the University of Texas at Brownsville and Texas Southmost College (UTB/TSC) South Padre Island Education Center. On January 9, 1987, the officer in charge of Station Port Isabel BMCS J. L. Cartmill recommended to the Eighth Coast Guard District commander

A sign in front of the old Coast Guard station reads, "UTB TSC South Padre Island Center," an indicator of its new purpose and mission. *USCG Station SPI collection.*

that an additional tract of land for student and administration parking be granted. This request was made to make a clear definition between Coast Guard property and college property. The building has been used repeatedly and offers continuing adult education courses, a testing center for computer certifications and evening classes for college students.

SHRIMP IMPORT LEGISLATION FOR SEA TURTLE CONSERVATION (1989)

The Coast Guard is responsible for enforcing all applicable federal laws on the waters that fall under United States jurisdiction, and protected species laws are no exception. In 1987, the federal regulations were published to require all U.S. shrimp boats to include turtle excluder devices (TEDs) on all nets being used.

A TED is a metal-barred circular device that is sown at an angle into the net's narrow neck. A deflection exit hole is made in the net at the point of deflection from the device, and any turtle that hits the bars will be deflected from going deeper into the cod end of the net; instead, they are discharged from the net through the deflection exit hole. The shrimp pass through the bars and are caught in the usual fashion for the shrimpers.

The TED enforcement was in response to the Kemp's ridley sea turtle being placed on the endangered species list. The TED device was created in an effort to keep turtles from being caught up in shrimpers' nets, causing them to drown before the nets are hauled in. Prior to this, there had been TEDs dating back to the 1970s, but it was on a volunteer and encouraged basis by the National Oceanic and Atmospheric Administration (NOAA) and the National Marine Fisheries Service (NMFS). In the Brazos Santiago Pass, there is a Port Isabel Shrimp Basin and a Brownsville Shrimp Basin that were home to between eight hundred and one thousand shrimp boats during the industry's peak. The largest responsibility of enforcing these federal regulations fell to the local Coast Guard unit and cutters. Coast Guard Station Port Isabel and the CGC *Point Nowell* worked closely with the local NMFS agents in enforcing these new federal regulations.

These new laws were not well received by the shrimping community, and at one point, defying the TED regulations had become an arrestable offense for the captain of a shrimp boat that was found to be in violation. In July 1988, the local shrimp boat owners protested by blocking the Brownsville Ship Channel, refusing to let any other traffic pass through the channel.

Opposite, top: A case file photograph documenting fisheries violations in South Texas. *USCG Station SPI collection.*

Opposite, bottom: The sign reads, "U.S. Coast Guard Border STOP," directing all inbound vessels to heave to for a Coast Guard inspection of fisheries and safety equipment. *USCG Station SPI collection.*

Above: The trailer on the barge allowed for a 24/7 immediate response by Coast Guard boarding officers and inspectors. *USCG Station SPI collection.*

Between ninety and one hundred shrimp boats lined up across the channel, shoulder to shoulder and several rows deep. Indeed, it was a sign of solidarity and unity in protesting what was felt to be unreasonable expectations by the federal government. This increased frustration with the federal agencies and inspectors involved and the other industries that utilize the Brownsville Ship Channel. The Coast Guard temporarily staged a "STOP barge" just inside the Brazos Santiago Pass, requiring all returning shrimp boats to stop alongside the barge for an inspection of all safety laws and of their TEDs.

The protest of the TEDs was that the device could also reduce the amount of shrimp that could be caught, cutting deeply into the already narrow profit margins of the shrimping community. Efforts to improve the TED were made over the years. In working with the federal agencies, especially Sea Grant Texas, the turtle excluder device was improved on to do a better job of keeping the shrimp while releasing the turtles.

CPOA, Rio Grande Chapter, Established in 1990

The rank of chief petty officer (CPO) in the U.S. Coast Guard was approved in 1920 by the sixty-sixth Congress of the United States. Station keepers of the life-saving service were given the rank position of chief boatswain's mate. The chief's anchor is a symbol that comes from the revenue cutter service. This titling of life-saving service members and combining traditions of the revenue cutter service paved the way for the newly named U.S. Coast Guard of 1915, when these two departments merged.

The chief petty officer is a critical leadership role today, as it was in its formative years. As a result of the high standards and leadership, associations were formed to further the chiefs' causes and responsibilities. Today, there are chief petty officer associations throughout the United States and its territories.

The idea of creating an association in the valley came as a result of the Coast Guard day picnic on August 6, 1990, with a gathering of a handful of retired chiefs. A list of the chiefs in the area was compiled, and a

The official certificate and seal recognizing the Rio Grande chapter of the Coast Guard Chief Petty Officers Association. It is signed by the national president, Frank Albright. *MKC B. Eason's collection.*

Family members gather to commemorate the RGV-CPOA, followed by a Texas-style barbeque. *MKC B. Eason's collection.*

mailing roster was created to solicit interest, and a petition to establish the Rio Grande Valley chapter was prepared. On August 15, Chief "Barnacle Bill" Eason drove three hours to Corpus Christi and hand delivered the paperwork to the national president of the CPOA QMC Frank Albright. The next day, August 16, the presentation was introduced to the twenty-second National CPOA Convention by Master Chief Doug Robertson. It was seconded and approved by all delegates, and as the motion passed, it received a standing ovation for having gone from concept to association in only ten days. On August 26, 1990, the national president of the CPOA made a memorable trip to South Padre Island to swear-in the newly elected officers. The ceremony was held on the forward deck of the CGC *Point Nowell*. MKC Bill Eason served as president, BMCM Ambrose Pechacek served as vice president, BMC Bob Felan served as secretary and LT Philip Kolb served as treasurer of the newly formed Rio Grande Valley Chief Petty Officers Association.

Operation Gulf Shield (1997)

Leading up to Operation Gulf Shield in 1994, the commandant of the Coast Guard Admiral Robert Kramek was placed in charge of the United States Interdiction and Counterdrug Operations. Under Admiral Kramek's leadership, Operation Frontier Shield was placed in the Caribbean, focusing on the eastern side.

The U.S. Interdiction and Counterdrug Operations had proven to be successful in deterring smuggling activities through Operation Frontier Shield in the Caribbean Islands. With this success, two more operations were planned, with a focus on the maritime border of the United States and Mexico—Operation Border Shield on the Pacific side and Operation Gulf Shield on the Gulf of Mexico side.

Operation Gulf Shield commenced in 1997, placing its command coordination center at Coast Guard Station Port Isabel, the southernmost station on the border with Mexico. The station was responsible for managing the influx and daily tasking of more than ninety-five crewmembers, as well as the U.S. Customs, the Drug Enforcement Agency, U.S. Border Patrol, JTF-6 and several Texas law enforcement agencies in support of Operation Gulf Shield. This was the largest multiagency law enforcement operation ever conducted on United States soil.

Bales of seized marijuana stacked in front of the Coast Guard station. *USCG Station SPI collection.*

U.S. Coast Guard ground and air support patrols Boca Chica Beach to the Rio Grande River's mouth on the Texas border. *USCG Station SPI collection.*

Coast Guard Station Port Isabel was responsible for identifying essential equipment and implementing an intelligence watch section that provided a common-link watch-relief process for eight separate operational units and provided the operations center at Air Station Corpus Christi with "real-time information in providing Operation Gulf Shield with air support."

It is important to note that while there was advanced technology utilized in the way of mobile radar units from the Texas governor's taskforce (Governor George W. Bush), U.S. Marine Corps Listening and Observation Posts (LPOPs), this was also the first time since World War II that the Coast Guard went back to the basics and implemented "beach patrols."

The Coast Guard issued a press release from the commandant of the Coast Guard on March 27, 1997:

TEXAS GOVERNOR BUSH AND COAST GUARD COMMANDANT KRAMEK ANNOUNCE MAOR GULF LAW ENFORCEMENT OPERATION

Corpus Christi, Texas—Texas Governor George W. Bush and Coast Guard Commandant and Untied States Interdiction Coordinator Admiral Robert E. Kramek today released details of OPERATION GULF SHIELD, a major, coordinated effort to deny drug smuggling routes into South Texas. This operation directly supports Goal #4 of President Clinton's National Drug Control Strategy, to shield America's air, land, and sea frontiers from the drug threat.

"Gulf Shield's objective is simple; deny the routes of traffickers…and disrupt their operations," Admiral Kramek said. "With Governor Bush's tremendous support, we've put together the right team to shield South Texas and the nation from this major drug threat."

This major law enforcement operation joins Cost Guard units in Texas, augmented by additional Coast Guard forces from around the nation and a range of federal and Texas State law enforcement organizations. Key agencies are the U.S. Border Patrol, Joint Task Force 6, Texas National Guard, Texas Air National Guard, Governor of Texas Covert Operations Response Team (CORE), U.S. Customs, Texas Parks & Wildlife, Cameron County Sheriff's Office & Task Force, and the Drug Enforcement Administration.

Coast Guard Rear Admiral Timothy Josiah, commander of the operation, said, "Gulf Shield is designed to project a large law enforcement presence in the remote area of Texas' Gulf Coast and border region of Mexico, through which an estimated 12 metric tons of cocaine and 125 metric tons of marijuana are shipped each year." Rear Admiral Josiah said that inter-agency forces will use a range of aircraft, ships, boats, land patrols, and sensors to detect and suppress illegal activity.

The drugs are brought into Texas by small, fast boats called "lanchas" 30+ knot capable boats that depart from Mexican ports and beaches. Usually operating under cover of darkness, or bad weather, the lanchas deliver their loads of cocaine and marijuana to remote beach areas north of the Rio Grande River and onto South Padre Island. The drugs are then picked up for land shipment throughout Texas and the U.S.

Approximately 700 personnel from the various federal, state and local agencies will participate in the operation. Gulf Shield is expected to run indefinitely.

For more information, contact the Group Corpus Christi Public Affairs Officer or Eighth District Public Affairs offices.

U.S. Coast Guard fast response RHIs teams in pursuit of suspect vessels. *BMC J. Epps's collection.*

A seized drug-smuggling vessel outfitted with a center console for training and counter-smuggling operations manned by U.S. Coast Guard boat crews. *BMC J. Epps's collection.*

The U.S. Coast Guard seized illegal fishing and drug-smuggling vessels. *Author's collection.*

The station received the following Coast Guard Meritorious Unit Commendation (CGMUC) within the first three months of Operation Gulf Shield:

For meritorious service during the period 1 January to 30 April 1997 in the planning and execution of Operation GULF SHIELD, a Coast Guard led, a multi-agency effort intended to deny the expanding narcotics and migrant smuggling route in the Gulf of Mexico along the Mexico/United States maritime border and to encourage enhanced maritime interdiction operation with Mexico. Under the operational control of commander, Eighth Coast Guard District, and tactical control of Commander, Group Corpus Christi, Operation GULF SHIELD was developed to interdict Mexican lanchas—small, fast open-hulled boats that smuggle an estimated 125 metric tons of marijuana and 12,000 kilograms of cocaine onto the beaches of South Padre Island each year. With the participation of six federal agencies, five state agencies, and the Department of Defense, Operation GULF SHIELD established new standards of inter-agency cooperation in counter-narcotics law enforcement operations. Coast Guard boats, cutters, and aircraft provided a continuous offshore presence, while shore-based radar and infrared imaging equipment, along with covert observation posts provided by the Texas National Guard and Joint Task Force Six, provided unparalleled surveillance. U.S. Special Forces command helped develop innovative small boat tactics designed to counter the speed and maneuverability of the lanchas. Texas law enforcement personnel from the Governor's office covert response team joined Coast Guard law enforcement detachment personnel to form Helicopter Response Teams to be airlifted to apprehend smugglers reaching shore. For the first time since World War II, Coast Guard personnel took to the beaches as part of a coastal watch, that in partnership with the Border Patrol, deterred the use of Boca Chica Beach as a destination for smugglers crossing the mouth of the Rio Grande River. This multi-agency task force proved its effectiveness during the first week of the operation when a combined Coast Guard and Border Patrol team surprised a lanchas on Boca Chic beach and seized its 1,085 pounds cargo of marijuana. Through its high-visibility presence, this operation has significantly disrupted the flow of narcotics into south Texas. The tactical and technical innovations developed for Operation GULF SHIELD laid a foundation for continued regional cooperation and inter-agency contribution to the

The original crew of Operation Gulf Shield receiving the CGMUC Award. *Author's collection.*

national drug control strategy. The significance of joint action by the Mexican Navy is demonstrated by an increased exchange of valuable intelligence and its proposal to the Mexican Commerce Department to regulate the use of large outboard engines on lanchas. The superb performance and devotion to duty demonstrated by Operation Gulf Shield Forces are in keeping with the highest traditions of the United States Coast Guard.

The Operational Distinguishing Device is authorized.

Within the first month of Operation Gulf Shield, it yielded a total of 6,300 pounds of marijuana, the seizure of two lanchas, two vehicles and the arrests of five people for trafficking narcotics.

COAST GUARD FOUNDATION HONORS STATION PORT ISABEL (1997)

Since 1969, the Coast Guard Foundation (CGF) has been a 501(c)(3) nonprofit organization that supports and honors the missions of the United States Coast Guard members. The mission of the CGF is to partner with the Coast Guard to provide resources to members and families to build resilience and strengthen the entire community. The vision of the CGF is a world in which all Coast Guard members and their families are valued and have the support they need to succeed throughout their lives. The values

An aerial view of the Station Port Isabel administration, barracks and waterfront facilities, circa 1997. *BMC J. Epps's collection.*

of the CGF drive everything it does to support Coast Guard members and their families.

The Coast Guard Foundation provides awards and recognitions for heroism and mission excellence. In 1997, Station Port Isabel received the Coast Guard Foundation Award for mission excellence:

> *R 14151Z Jul 1997 ZUI ASN-CH0195000025*
> *FM ALLD8UNITS*
> *R 141355Z JUL 97 ZUI ASN-D08195000263*
> *FM COMDT COGARD WASHINGTON DC/ /G-W/ /*
> *TO ALDIST*
> *BT*
> *UNCLAS / /N01650*
> *ALDIST 166/97*
> *COMDTNOT 1650*
> *SUBJ: ANNOUNCEMENT OF COAST GUARD*
> *FOUNDATION AWARD SELECTEES*
> *…*
> *C. Coast Guard Station Port Isabel, Texas—Other Missions.*
> *Station Port Isabel is being recognized for its performance during a*
> *heightened tempo of operations, including prosecution of over 250*
> *SAR cases, saving 4 lives and assisting 364 people, conducting 343*
> *CFVSR boardings and seizing over $7.3 million in contraband.*

The Coast Guard Foundation Awards Ceremony in New York City. Station Port Isabel crew members with the commandant of the Coast Guard Admiral Kramek. *Author's collection.*

Their law enforcement efforts precipitated the highly acclaimed U.S. Customs Operation White Shark and the Coast Guard's ongoing Operation Gulf Shield.

…

Please pass my congratulations to all…

BT

NNNN

****

*   *UNCLASSIFIED*   *

****

The old and dilapidated waterfront building in need of much repair and replacement. *PSC JC Chapa's collection.*

COAST GUARD BOATHOUSE AND WATERFRONT PROJECT (1998)

In 1998, a $3.2 million waterfront project was completed and included new office space, ready rooms with lockers, showers and restrooms. The seawall was reinforced, and a covered mooring was added as well as new docks and mooring facilities. Today, some of this space houses the administrative offices of the aids to navigation team and the cutters that are homeported on South Padre Island.

STATION PORT ISABEL, RENAMED STATION SOUTH PADRE ISLAND (1998)

Station Port Isabel was physically located on South Padre Island. To get to Station Port Isabel, one had to pass through the town of Port Isabel and continue for another three miles over the causeway bridge to the southern end of South Padre Island. In an effort to properly align the station's name to where it was physically located, in 1998, the station was renamed Coast Guard Station South Padre Island.

MARINE PROTECTOR–CLASS CUTTERS (2001)

The marine protector–class patrol boats, named after marine predators such as *Amberjack*, *Alligator* and *Cormorant*, were put into service in an effort to

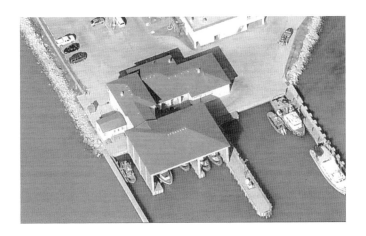

Top: An aerial view of the new waterfront facility, including the covered docks, ready rooms with showers and engineering and deck force spaces. *USCG Station SPI collection.*

Middle: The covered docks facility from the waterside of the station seawall and vessel entrance. *USCG Station SPI collection.*

Bottom: The official building plaque commemorating the waterfront project's completion and the renaming of the station to Station South Padre Island. *Author's collection.*

CGC *Amberjack* (WPB-87315) moored at South Padre Island. *USCG Station SPI collection.*

An aerial view of the CGC *Cormorant* (WPB-87313) underway at high speed. Note the stern launch/recovery feature of the RHI small boat. *USCG Station SPI collection.*

The CGC *Alligator* (WPB-87372) moored at South Padre Island with its dress ship flags hoisted. *USCG Station SPI collection.*

relieve and replace the aging eighty-two-foot-long Point-class patrol boats. The marine protector–class vessels are five feet longer than the Point-class cutters (*Point Nowell* and *Point Baker*) at eighty-seven feet long. The extra five feet paved the way for a safer and faster response time in launching and recovering the rigged-hull inflatable (RHI) boats carried by them. The Point-class cutter utilized a crane and boat cradle that sat on the main deck aft of the superstructure. The marine protector–class vessels have a built-in stern launching ramp that is quicker and safer to launch and recover the RHI boats by crewmembers.

A total of seventy-four marine protector–class cutters have been placed into service. The CGC *Amberjack* was the first to serve on the Texas border and was replaced by the CGC *Cormorant*, which was replaced by the CGC *Alligator*.

CAUSEWAY BRIDGE COLLAPSE (SEPTEMBER 15, 2001)

On the emergency maritime radio channel, channel 16 came the desperate cry for help that would prove to be one of the deadliest maritime disasters in modern times in South Texas. A tugboat wheelman calling, "Mayday, mayday, mayday," reported that vehicles were falling into the water on the early morning of Saturday, September 15, 2001, as reported by the Port of Brownsville guard log.

Mayday is an emergency term to indicate that help is needed, as there is a life-threatening emergency. In response to the mayday call, Coast Guard Air Station Corpus Christi responded and dispatched aircraft and station South Padre Island rescue boats. The CGC *Mallet*, an aids to navigation vessel that was working locally in the Port Mansfield area, responded. Local police, EMS and fire services from South Padre Island, Port Isabel, Brownsville and Los Fresnos also responded. The Coast Guard Marine Safety Detachment Brownsville and Coast Guard Auxiliary Flotilla 7-2 responded. But it was too late, the damage had been done.

On the previous Friday night, a little after 9:00 p.m., a tugboat with a load of four loaded hopper barges ahead of it in a single file straight line (*strung-out* is the familiar mariner's term) got underway from its moorings up the Brownsville Ship Channel and was proceeding to the Intracoastal Waterway, eastbound. The four end-to-end barges are approximately 800 feet long, 35 feet wide and, when loaded, had a deep draft of approximately 9 feet and 3 inches. The wheelman who was navigating the tugboat and barges, at approximately 1:45 a.m., passed through the Long Island Swing Bridge, and about fifteen minutes later, hit the Causeway Bridge almost

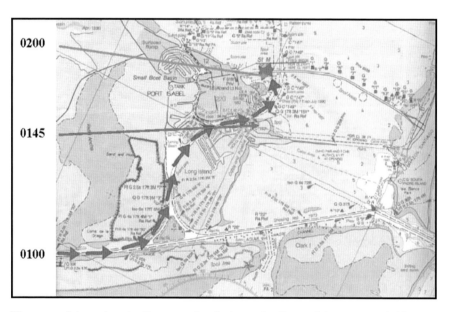

The route of the tugboat leading up to the allusion and collapse of the causeway bridge. *USCG Station SPI collection.*

The CGC *Mallet* was the Coast Guard–designated on-scene-commander. *USCG Station SPI collection.*

head-on in what turned out to be approximately 375 feet west of the channel. The Causeway Bridge is the only bridge between Port Isabel and South Padre Island, and it is approximately two and a half miles long.

As a result of the collision, two eighty-foot-long sections of the highway collapsed, leaving a gaping hole where a bridge once was. Nine vehicles entered the water through the missing bridge section, resulting in the loss of eight lives and three injuries. Later that day, during rescue and recovery operations, a third eighty-foot-long section of the bridge also collapsed.

The first to contact the tugboat operator was Coast Guard Chief Warrant Officer Alan Grodecki, the supervisor of the Coast Guard marine safety detachment in Brownsville. Testimony of the event that night indicated that loaded barges such as these present less sail area to be affected by the wind, and because more of the barges were below the water surface, they were affected more by the water current. The weather conditions reported the tide at 2.19 feet above mean lower low tide at 0200 local time (incoming). The helmsman indicated that after he went through the Long Island Swing Bridge, he began making the S-curve turn toward the Causeway Bridge when the starboard stern of the tugboat hit bottom or something on the bottom. His impression was that this hit or bump caused him to lose control of the configuration, which was then overwhelmed by a starboard-to-port current.

The Coast Guard aids to navigation team, South Padre Island, conducted a post-casualty survey of the aids to navigation in the area on September 15 and found that all of the relevant Coast Guard aids were on station and watching properly.

The helmsman reported that the green centering lights hanging beneath the bridge in the center of the channel were not working but that the red fender lights were working, indicating where the channel passed through the bridge.

In 2003, the bridge was renamed the Queen Isabella Memorial Bridge to honor those lives lost.

RESCUE 21 COMMUNICATIONS (2012)

In 2009, in an effort to update search-and-rescue communications throughout the United States, the idea of a communication system upgrade called Rescue 21 was being considered in South Texas. In 2012, in an effort to modernize the rescue communications systems in Texas, a four-hundred-foot remote fixed facility (RFF) tower was installed on Coast Guard property on South Padre Island. It is a modern tower that requires no guide wires, and it is self-supported with a lattice engineered–style design. At the top of the tower is a direction finding (DF) antenna that helps locate distressed mariners through their radio signal.

The historic station can be seen in the foreground, and the four-hundred-foot-tall Rescue 21 RFF tower is in the background. A symbol of old meets the new and continues with the mission—Semper Paratus! *USCG Station SPI collection.*

The Rescue 21 allows the Coast Guard to monitor voice transmission on emergency channels and determine potential mariners' location line in distress. The tower was designated as a remote fixed facility (RFF) on South Padre Island, making it the southernmost RFF Rescue 21 tower in Texas. The nearest RFF tower is north of Cameron County, in Kenedy County, and it is designated as the RFF Kenedy Tower. The South Padre Island Rescue 21 RFF tower stands between the current Coast Guard station of 1974 and the old historic Coast Guard station of 1928.

5

The Future of the Coast Guard

Twenty-First Century

L ooking back gives one pause to think about the future. What once started out under the leadership of Alexander Hamilton and the Department of Treasury is, today, one of the world's premier organizations, now proudly serving under the Department of Homeland Security—the United States Coast Guard.

The mission is ever-changing along the Texas border. In the 1800s, they rowed man-powered rescue boats through the surf. Today, the latest technology that propels rescue teams through the surf is sophisticated, impressive and computerized. In the twenty-first century, new missions include working on evolving environmental issues and law enforcement and search-and-rescue missions.

In the last twenty years, new missions have created new positions (ratings): maritime enforcement specialist, operations specialist, intelligence specialist, information systems technician, diver and investigator. The maritime enforcement specialist position was created in response to the ever-growing demand for enforcing the laws by the U.S. Coast Guard. Prior to this, marine law enforcement was a collateral duty assignment that graduates of marine law enforcement class C schools were assigned to, and oftentimes, it fell on members of the boat crew, such as boatswain's mates and machinery technicians. A dedicated maritime enforcement specialist rating provides dedicated informed individuals who enforce the laws and conduct inspections on the high seas and federal waterways.

In the 1940s, a crew of fourteen; in the 1980s, a crew of thirty-two; today, a crew of sixty-five men and women stand ready to proudly serve on the Texas border. *USCG Station SPI collection.*

The operations specialist position came about from forming the radarman rate and the telecommunications specialist rate requirements into this new rating. The operations specialists work the planning and execution of search-and-rescue cases and law enforcement operations, intelligence-gathering missions and with other intelligence agencies such as the Federal Bureau of Investigation, U.S. Customs and U.S. Border Patrol.

The intelligence specialist collects and gathers data, analyzes information from various collection points and other agencies to complement Coast Guard leadership and decisions for real-time events. The intelligence specialists prepare and present at briefings critical findings that support mission effectiveness.

The information systems technician position came about by combining the telecommunications specialist and the telephone technician ratings. As technology has increased, so has the demand to maintain it. Communication technology in the way of computer systems and networking is the primary field for which the information systems technician rating was created.

The investigator rating is a Coast Guard Reserve rating that was created to support the intelligence and law enforcement maritime missions. The investigators complete background checks, perform criminal investigations and provide personal protection services to senior Coast Guard officers.

The diver rating was created to support the Coast Guard's other missions, such as security, salvage, inspections, environmental, aids to navigation and polar ice operations. As well as being equally important, the Coast Guard divers work in joint operations with other U.S. and international military dive teams.

Arguably the oldest rate in the Coast Guard is that of boatswain's mate—sailor, a jack of all trades and master of none. It is the only enlisted rating that is allowed to serve in command positions as an officer in charge (OIC) or executive petty officer (XPO) of stations and cutters for multi-missions. This dates back to 1915, when the life-saving service merged into the U.S. Coast Guard. The station keepers were designated as boatswain's mates.

While the future of the Coast Guard is not known, it is clear that as long as there are safety and law enforcement boardings to be done, drug trafficking to be stopped, ports and waterways to be protected, marine inspections and investigations to be completed and lives to be saved, the Coast Guard will always be here, always ready to answer the call—Semper Paratus.

> *We're always ready for the call,*
> *We place our trust in Thee.*
> *Through surf and storm and howling gale,*
> *High shall our purpose be.*
> *"Semper Paratus" is our guide,*
> *Our fame, our glory, too.*
> *To fight to save or fight and die,*
> *Aye! Coast Guard we are for you!*
> *—U.S. Coast Guard fight song*

List of Abbreviations

AOR: area of operation
ANB: aids to navigation boat
A-to-N: aids to navigation
ATON: aids to navigation team
BMCM: master chief boatswain's mate
BZ: Bravo and Zulu, nautical signal flags flown vertically, means "well done."
CGC: Coast Guard cutter
CGF: Coast Guard Foundation
CMUC: Coast Guard Meritorious Unit Commendation
CPO: chief petty officer
CPOA: Chief Petty Officer's Association
CWO: chief warrant officer
DF: direction finder
LCDR: lieutenant commander
LORAN: long-range navigation
LT: lieutenant
LTJG: lieutenant, junior grade
MHS: United States Marine Hospital Service
MKC: chief machinery technician
MLB: motor lifeboat
MSD: marine safety detachment
MSM: Meritorious Service Medal
POB: persons on board

QMC: chief quartermaster
RFF: remote fixed facility
SAR: search and rescue
USCG: United States Coast Guard
USLSS: United States Life-Saving Service
WPB: hull designation, Point-class patrol boat
WPC: hull designation, Sentinel-class fast response cutter
WSC: hull designation, Active-class patrol boat

Bibliography

Alperin, L.M. *History of the Gulf Intracoastal Waterway*. Washington, D.C.: U.S. Army Engineers Water Resources Support Center, 1983. www.doczz.net.

Bates, Rod. *Historic Port Isabel: A Guide to Port Isabel's History, Dining, Shopping and Entertainment*. Port Isabel, TX: Port Isabel Museums, n.d.

Bates, Valerie. *Port Isabel*. Charleston, SC: Arcadia Publishing, 2013.

Beard, Tom, and Walter Cronkite. *The Coast Guard*. N.p.: Universe Pub, 2010.

Bennett, Robert F. *The Coast Guardsman's Manual*. Annapolis, MD: U.S. Naval Institute Press, 1983.

Chilton, Carl. "A History of the Development of Brazos Santiago Pass." In *Further Studies in Rio Grande Valley History*. Vol. 7. The UTB/TSC Regional History Series. Edited by Milo Kearney, Anthony Knopp and Antonio Zavaleta. Brownsville: University of Texas at Brownsville and Texas Southmost College, 2006, 75–80.

Dart, Andrew K. Raymondville LORAN History. www.ae5d.com.

Dietz, Bill. LORAN History. www.loran-history.info.

Dring, Timothy R. *U.S. Life-Saving Service and U.S. Coast Guard Stations Located Along the Gulf of Mexico Coastlines of Florida, Louisiana and Texas, and Their Assigned Stations Rescue Boats*. Washington, D.C.: U.S. Coast Guard, 2016.

Great Lakes Naval Memorial and Museum. www.silversidesmuseum.org.

Hall, R.S. *Lighthouses, Lightships, and Beacons of Texas: A Comprehensive Field Guide*. Houston, TX: Pintail Publishing, 2012.

Hildebrand, Walter W. "The History of Cameron County, Texas." Master's thesis, University of North Texas, 1950. www.digital.library.unt.edu.

Ireland, John (governor). "Quarantine Proclamation by the Governor of Texas, 1884." Library of Congress. www.hdl.loc.gov.

Jerrod, Michael, and Bender Thomas. "Fighting Smallpox on the Texas Border: An Episode from PHS's Proud Sage Publications." 1984. www.jstor.org.

Kearney, Milo, Anthony Knopp and Antonio Zavaleta. *Studies in Matamoros and Cameron County History*. Edinburg, TX: University of Texas Rio Grande Valley, 1997.

Kieslich, James. "A Case History of Port Mansfield Channel, Texas." Army Corps of Engineers, general investigation of tidal inlets report no. 12, 1977.

Koski-Karell, Daniel, Melissa Wiedenfeld, Chad Blackwell, Marjorie Nowick, Kathryn Plimpton and Lori Vermass. "U.S. Government Life-Saving Stations, Houses of Refuge, and Pre-1950 U.S. Coast Guard Lifeboat Stations." National Register of Historic Places, multiple property documentation form. United States Department of the Interior, National Park Service, 2013

Leatherwood Art. "Brazos Santiago, TX." *Handbook of Texas Online*. www.tshaonline.org.

———. "Port Mansfield Channel." *Handbook of Texas Online*. www.tshaonline.org.

Light, Jere C. "A History of Fishing in South Texas." In S*tudies in Rio Grande Valley History*. Vol. 6. The UTB/TSC Regional History Series. Edited by Milo Kearney, Anthony Knopp and Antonio Zavaleta. Brownsville, TX: University of Texas at Brownsville and Texas Southmost College, 2006, 61–65.

Marshall, Amy. *A History of Buoys and Tenders*. Washington, D.C.: Coast Guard Historians Office, 1995.

McDougal, Steph. *Lighthouses of Texas*. Charleston, SC: Arcadia Publishing, 2014.

NOAA. *History of Turtle Excluder Devices*. https://www.fisheries.noaa.gov/southeast/bycatch/history-turtle-excluder-devices 2019. Accessed on Mar 25, 2021.

Port Isabel Economic Development Corporation. "A Brief History of Port Isabel." www.portisabel-texas.com.

Texas State Historical Association. Handbook of Texas Online. www.tshaonline.org.

Thiesen, William. "Pablo Valent, Mariano Holland and Indalecio Lopez: Hispanic-American Lifesavers and the Florida Keys Hurricane of 1919," *Coast Guard Compass*, October 4, 2010. www.coastguard.dodlive.mil.

Tilley, John A. *The United States Coast Guard Auxiliary: A History, 1939–1999.* Washington, D.C.: U.S. Coast Guard, 2003. www.babel.hathitrust.org.

URS Group. *Historic Context Study of the United States Coast Guard in Sector Corpus Christi, from Port Aransas South to the Rio Grande, Brownsville Texas.* Washington, D.C.: United States Coast Guard, 2014.

U.S. Coast Guard. "Formal Investigation into the Circumstances Surrounding the Allison Between a Barge Tow and the Queen Isabell Causeway Bridge on September 15, 2001, in Port Isabel, Texas Resulting in Multiple Loss of Life." 2005. www.dco.uscg.mil.

———. "United States Coast Guard at War: Beach Patrol." 1945. www.media.defense.gov.

U.S. Coast Guard Atlantic Area. www.atlanticarea.uscg.mil.

U.S. Coast Guard Aviation History. "1996—Drug Interdiction Surge Operations Re-established." www.cgaviationhistory.org.

U.S. Coast Guard Chief Petty Officers Association (CPOA). www.uscgcpoa.org.

U.S. Coast Guard Historian's Office. www.history.uscg.mil.

U.S. Coast Guard History Program. "Brazos Station Texas." www.media.defense.gov.

USLSSHA United States Life-Saving Service Heritage Association. www.uslife-savingservice.org.

Willoughby, Malcom. *Rum War at Sea.* Washington, D.C.: Government Printing Office, 1964.

Wooldridge, Ruby, and Deolece Farmelee. *The 1923 Point Isabel Coast Guard Building.* San Benito, TX: N.p., n.d.

Index

About the Author

Dr. Jackie Kyger is a university professor and a retired Coast Guard officer. He spent much of his career on border initiatives, in the way of search-and-rescue, law enforcement and counter–narcotics trafficking and human smuggling. Chief Warrant Officer Jackie Kyger proudly served at the following Coast Guard units along the Texas border, and these experiences were his inspiration for this collection of visual history:

- Auxiliary (Flotilla 7-2), Boat-Coxswain.
- Station South Padre Island, Commanding Officer.
- Station Port Isabel, Commanding Officer.
- Port Mansfield, Aids to Navigation Team, Officer in Charge.
- CGC *Point Nowell* (WPB-82636), Executive Petty Officer.
- Reserve Unit Port Isabel, Station Keeper.
- Station Port Isabel, Boat-Coxswain.

He is an alumnus of Texas A&M University, Kingsville, holding a doctorate in education. He is a plank owner of the National Coast Guard Museum. Dr. Kyger is a leading member and volunteer of the Community of Christ Historic Sites Foundation's Oral History Program. He was awarded the Meritorious Service Medal for his leadership as commanding officer of Station South Padre Island.

He resides in South Texas, where he is active in promoting local history as a storyteller, author and novelist.